GEORGE MÜLLER AND HIS ORPHANS

This book tells the incredible story of George Müller who, born in Germany in 1805, came to England when he was 23 and in 1836 founded his first orphanage. In his lifetime he founded five homes and sheltered thousands of orphans. Every penny for their support came entirely from unsolicited gifts of money or kind. No appeals—public or private— were made and no advertisements were put out. All help came in answer to prayer by Müller and his supporters, with their unshakeable faith. The work continued after his death. Today, of course, there is no need for such residential homes but the help continues by way of day centres, family care centres and there is even a home for the elderly.

GEORGE MÜLLER AND HIS ORPHANS

Nancy Garton

With an introduction by The Right Rev John Bickersteth, former Bishop of Bath and Wells

CHIVERS PRESS
BATH

First published in Great Britain 1963
by
Hodder & Stoughton
This Large Print edition published by
Chivers Press
by arrangement with
the author
1992

ISBN 0 7451 1675 2

British Library Cataloguing in Publication Data available

And here we give thee most high praise and hearty thanks for all thy Saints, who have been the chosen vessels of thy grace, and lights of the world in their several generations; and we pray, that rejoicing in their fellowship, and following their good examples, we may be partakers with them of thy heavenly kingdom. (From: The Prayer for the Church Militant. *Book of Common Prayer as proposed in 1928.*)

FOREWORD

BY
The Right Rev. John Bickersteth
Former Bishop of Bath and Wells

'A pioneer among orphanages' the author calls George Müller's five houses on Ashley Down, Bristol, and this book bears out what she claims. Whereas today it is easy to brand the orphanage concept as Victorian patronising *par excellence*, the fact remains that the alternative for these abandoned children was in those days pauperism, degradation and misery. You have only to read how the beneficiaries themselves later viewed their early years under George Müller's care to be convinced that his institutions were not the unloving barrack-like places of some people's imagination.

Without any question the atmosphere that old boys and girls gratefully remember was a Christian atmosphere, born, as Nancy Garton says, of 'love for God and love for man'. Prayer and thanksgiving were part and parcel of the life there.

So this book is very much a testament to the power of prayer. My goodness, the Müllers and the staff did pray; their consuming passion was that the boys and girls should come to know God through faith in Christ. Their example and their teaching were all geared to that end. George himself prayed in every circumstance and for every need—for staff, for food, for money—and his needs were always met. Emotionally a very unEnglish German, though by the time he was sixty a naturalised Englishman, he would let himself go in both the spoken and written word, and people all over the world (he did no less than seventeen tours, travelling 200,000 miles in all kinds of conditions) warmed to his compassion and his love. Totally unsectarian in his outlook, he accepted invitations to preach in any church where the teaching was Bible-based; it would be interesting to know where that principle would take him today; certainly right across the denominations. He was as convinced of the rightness of receiving the Sacrament every Sunday as he was of believers' baptism; minister of Ebenezer Chapel in Teignmouth, he was married in an Anglican church in Exeter; and as myself a former curate of a Bristol church in the '50s when the Müller homes as they came to be called were still very much in action. I am glad to be invited to write a foreword to the reprint of this fine record of a remarkable Christian, whose philanthropic vision brought fulfilled lives to many thousands of deprived children. Müller's work is an important part of English social history during the past 150 years.

John Bath and Wells

'The story by Nancy Garton brought tears to my eyes; many parts in it are so real and touching. If she had been one of the girls herself she couldn't have described our lives more accurately.'

An Old Girl of the Müller Homes

CONTENTS

CONTENTS

PREFACE

I am not myself a member of that part of the Church of which George Müller was a leader. Being the daughter of one Anglican clergyman and the wife of another, I live and hope to die a member of the Church of England. Yet who, discerning the family likeness in all of God's saints, does not at times feel that the divisions of Christendom are unreal. However much we may love the denomination that has nurtured us, it is surely the Holy Church Universal that has the over-riding claim to our loyalty.

I first heard of the subject of this biography many years ago, but closer acquaintance began when an old Müller boy lent me his copy of *The Autobiography of George Müller*. That bulky volume is not to be assimilated in one casual reading, but as I studied it over a long period, Müller's remarkable personality and amazing career began to impress itself upon me. It was soon after we moved to a parish not far from Bristol that the urge came to me to write his life story, and with it the realisation that geographically I was now in the ideal situation to attempt the task. With the Müller Homes and so many people connected with them so easily accessible, I could obtain first-hand information. I was able, too, to visit No. 3 Orphan House on

Ashley Down, see over it and try to absorb its atmosphere. The great building was about to pass into other hands. Had I waited another month I should have been too late. Even a day's delay would have meant seeing over an Orphan House bereft of children, as the very next day the few remaining ones departed to their new Home in Cotham, Bristol. The majority had moved away some time before. This gave me the feeling of having been led there just in time to achieve the purpose of gaining material for this book. It was still possible to get a good impression of the old schoolrooms, dormitories and playrooms.

All of those with whom I came in contact were extremely kind and helpful. The present Director, Mr. J. J. Rose, has given me more than one long interview, as well as supplying me with information by letter and telephone. I should like to express my gratitude to him, and also to his secretary, Miss Mary Muxworthy, who has searched through old records for me, and spent time showing me the exhibits in the little museum at Müller House.

My thanks are also due to the following, with all of whom I had lengthy and informative conversations: Mrs. H. Rendle-Short; Mr. Ronald Packer and Miss Packer; Mr. L. F. Gobey; Mr. W. Tidball and the late Mrs. Tidball; the late Captain L. Millidge; and Miss Grace Norwood. Lastly, I wish to thank Messrs. Pickering and Inglis for permission to quote

xiv

passages from their book, *George Müller of Bristol*.

George Müller was born at Kroppenstaedt, near Halberstadt, in Prussia, on September 27th, 1805 (one month before the Battle of Trafalgar).

In 1810 the Müller family moved to Heimersleben, four miles away.

George attended the Cathedral Classical School at Halberstadt from ten years old until sixteen. He was then sent to the Gymnasium at Nordhausen for two and a half years. He entered Halle University in 1825.

He came to England in 1829, and settled in Teignmouth in 1830.

He married Mary Groves on October 7th, 1830.

He and his wife moved to Bristol on May 25th, 1832. At first they shared a house with their friends the Craiks, then they lived at 6 Wilson Street (which eventually became the first Orphan House), then at 21 Paul Street, which has since been demolished. After the death of his second wife, Müller lived in No. 3 Orphan House on Ashley Down, and died there on March 10th, 1898.

George Müller became a naturalized Englishman on December 18th, 1861.

Herr Müller, his father, an Excise Collector. Died in 1840.

Frau Müller, his mother. Died 1819, or 1820.

A younger brother, Christian name not recorded. Died in 1838.

A much younger half-brother, Christian name not recorded.

Mary Groves, who became the first Mrs. Müller. Born about 1799, married October 7th, 1830, died 1870.

Lydia, their daughter. Born 1832, married 1871, died 1890. No children.

Elijah, their son. Born 1834, died the following year, aged 1 month.

James Wright, Müller's son-in-law and co-director. Died 1905.

Susannah Grace Sangar, who became the second Mrs. Müller, November, 1871. Died 1894.

The Narrative was an autobiographical account of Müller's early life, his conversion, and his work afterwards. It subsequently ran to four volumes, now out of print.

The Autobiography of George Müller was not an autobiography in the strict sense. It was a massive tome of 730 pages, compiled after Müller's death by his successor, Frederic Bergin. The material for it was drawn from the four volumes of the *Narrative*, with additional matter including an account of Müller's death and funeral, personal tributes to him in the Press and elsewhere being quoted at length. It contained over thirty large photographs of the Orphans and the Orphan Houses, and of Müller himself, his family and friends, and various places in Germany connected with his early life. It is now out of print.

The Reports. These are the Annual Reports of the Orphan Work and other Objects of the Scriptural Knowledge Institution, and have been published every year since 1839. They give a month-by-month account of the gifts in money and kind sent in answer to prayer, particularly of those in whose arrival there is anything significant or remarkable. The *Reports* have always been an essential feature because George Müller's primary intention in founding the Orphan Houses was to prove that God hears and answers prayer, and the *Reports* provided the means by which this could be demonstrated. Donors' names were never mentioned; merely the sum of money or the article in kind, with the name of the town from which they were sent, being stated. Statistics about the Orphan Houses were given, with a few pages of description of the children's routine, education, etc.

The Directors of the Scriptural Knowledge Institution, which includes the Orphan Houses, from 1836 to 1985 have been as follows:

George Müller.
James Wright.
Frederic G. Bergin.

THE MÜLLER HOMES TODAY

As a result of the 1948 Children's Act, the Trustees decided, after much prayer, to sell the five Orphan Houses on Ashley Down and buy smaller properties. Before 1960 the great houses had all been closed, and the 200 or so remaining children accommodated in 12 Family Group Homes in Bristol, Clevedon and Weston-super-Mare; the complete change-over having taken several years to effect. The enormous buildings were all purchased by the Local Authority and became the Bristol College of Technology. The Family Group Homes were each staffed by Houseparents and two assistants, and averaged twelve children in each home. However, in recent years the general policy nationwide has been away from residential homes, and instead, where possible to help children in need in their own homes. The Directors of the Müller Homes have seen the children's work in its traditional form drawing rapidly to a close.

Yet the plight of under-privileged children is no less real in today's society, so new ventures to help them are now being undertaken.

A Day Care Centre has been opened in one of the former Children's Homes, 'Glandore' in Weston-super-Mare. Thirty children can be looked after daily by Christian girls, Nursery Nurse trained. Sixty children are cared for each week, and there is a waiting list. But there is another type of centre, started in 1983—a Family Support Centre—which has proved so successful that by 1986 five had been opened at Bristol and Weston-super-Mare. These bring in the whole family, including the parents, on a daily basis, and so the family can be helped on a much deeper level in their relationships and with any emotional and above all, with any spiritual needs they may have. When necessary, mothers can learn to cook and to cope with other household matters, and are counselled in child care.

In November, 1983, the Müller Homes for the Elderly were officially registered with the Charity Commissioners. As usual in such cases, the Müller Trustees are not allowed to use either funds or buildings that have been given for the children's work for this new object. However, the Directors write (from the Müller Offices at 7 Cotham Park, Bristol), 'We are looking to the Lord to meet the substantial needs of this new charity, as He has in the past met the needs of the children, and still does today'.

'Tilsley House', the first of these Homes for the Elderly, which is at Weston-super-Mare, was opened in April, 1986. One of the residents, Miss Grace Norwood, who as one of the orphan girls is mentioned in the end chapters of this book, says: 'Living at Müller's is like coming home. They looked after me at the start, and now they are looking after me at the end.'

GEORGE MÜLLER AND HIS ORPHANS

CHAPTER ONE

SCHOOLBOY AND STUDENT

George Müller founded the five world-famous Orphan Houses on Ashley Down in Bristol, and for this reason he is often thought of chiefly as a philanthropist. Yet his philanthropy was really a by-product of the great purpose to which he devoted his life, which was, to strengthen the faith of Christians everywhere by demonstrating that God hears and answers prayer. Had his sole objective been to rescue orphan children from destitution, to feed, clothe, educate and bring them up as Christians, no doubt he would have done as Dr. Barnardo did, and appealed to the public for funds by large-scale advertising. He certainly did work unremittingly for the welfare of the orphans in his care, and every one of them was dear to him. Nevertheless, his chief and primary purpose in founding and maintaining those Orphan Houses was to give to all who had eyes to perceive it a visible proof that God is now and always the living God, responding to the prayers of all who trust in Him.

The story of this amazing man is full of paradoxes. In a sense he is inimitable, but it is also true, as he himself constantly asserted, that

1

what he did others may do, if they, too, look for answers to their prayers. Indeed, his helpers at the Orphan Houses, and his and their successors in the sixty and more years since his death, who have remained true to his principles and looked to God alone for supplies, have had their prayers answered as he did. The same is true of the many others, in various parts of the world, who have been inspired by his example to found orphanages and other charitable institutions run on his principles of faith and prayer. Seldom can any human being have been so successful in what he set out to do as was George Müller. He determined to show, with God's help, that faith and prayer really work, and he achieved his purpose so completely that his name has become almost a synonym for the prayer of faith.

His story begins on September 27th, 1805, with his birth at Kroppenstaedt in Prussia.

In the autobiographical record, which he called *The Narrative of the Lord's dealings with George Müller*, from which the facts concerning his early life as related in this present book are all drawn, he tells us very little about his mother, but his father, however, is mentioned in connection with various incidents which throw light on the characters of both father and son. Herr Müller, though in many ways an able man, appears to have been strangely gullible. For instance, he would entrust his two small sons with considerable amounts of cash to teach them to acquire the habit of possessing ready money without spending it. This led them both into frequent wrong-doing. George in particular devised numerous schemes for putting the money to his own use without being detected. Having squandered some, he would either falsify his accounts, or else count out what remained incorrectly in front of his father. Found out after a time and punished, he merely tried other ruses. Before he was ten years old he repeatedly stole from the government funds in his father's keeping. But one day Herr Müller, who had become suspicious by so constantly missing money, left him alone in a room in which was a counted sum. When the father returned, coins were, as usual, missing from the pile. They turned up, on search being made, in George's shoe.

He was punished again, but this did nothing to deter him. His only reaction was to contrive subtler methods to avoid discovery.

Herr Müller's plan for his elder son's future was that he should be a clergyman; in view of the boy's behaviour, of all careers surely the most unsuitable. However, his admitted reason for the choice makes it seem less incredible. It was in order that George might have a good living, with a comfortable parsonage in which his father might spend his declining years.

George certainly does not appear to have let

the prospect of such a serious profession weigh very heavily on his mind. He spent his schoolboy years in what he later describes collectively as 'sinful practices'.

The two brothers were the more exposed to temptation when they became day boys at the Cathedral Classical School at Halberstadt, arrangements being made for them to live in lodgings, with apparently little supervision in their free time. When George was fourteen, Frau Müller died. Not aware even that she was ill, on the Saturday he played cards until long after midnight, and on the Sunday went to a tavern with some of his companions, after which they all roamed the streets, intoxicated. On the Monday he attended his first confirmation class, but paid little heed to what was being taught. In the Lutheran Church confirmation has always been a great feature, to be preceded by a long series of classes lasting for months. But this, the first that George attended, must have been memorable if only by reason of the shock awaiting him on his return to his lodgings. Herr Müller was there, come to take his two sons home to their mother's funeral. But this bereavement made no lasting impression upon the older boy, and he became steadily worse.

There was a custom for candidates, on the eve of confirmation, to make a formal confession of their sins to the clergyman in the vestry. Müller relates that he made of this an opportunity to cheat the clergyman of eleven-twelfths of the fee which his father had given him.

The day of the confirmation is perhaps best given in his own words, as they provide the first evidence of the stirring of the Holy Spirit within him. He was fourteen-and-a-half years old.

'In this state of heart, without prayer, without true repentance, without faith, without knowledge of the plan of salvation, I was confirmed and took the Lord's Supper on the Sunday after Easter, 1820. Yet I was not without some feeling of the solemnity of the thing, and I stayed at home in the afternoon and evening, whilst the other boys and girls, who had been confirmed with me, walked about in the fields. I also made resolutions to turn from the vices in which I was living, and to study more. But as I attempted the thing in my own strength, all soon came to nothing, and I still grew worse.' George Müller made his first Communion in the Protestant Cathedral at Halberstadt.

The period from 1820 until 1825 was spent partly at school, partly in reading with tutors, but all the time in contriving, either by cajoling or by deceiving his father, to get his own way and to provide himself with money which was spent on dissipations. On one occasion, when

5

he was sixteen, having stayed for amusement at a hotel without the means to pay, he found himself in jail. He spent a miserable three weeks there, and was not released until Herr Müller had been informed and had dispatched money to redeem his debts. On reaching home George was given a good beating, and being by this time more than ordinarily subdued, he applied himself to study with unusual application, and soon restored himself to his father's favour.

Throughout these years the boy was perpetually, in a half-hearted way, wishing to be better, and made many resolutions which soon came to nothing. Later, during his student years, he rated the works of Horace and Cicero, Voltaire and Molière considerably above the Bible, of which he did not even possess a copy, though he owned about three hundred other books.

Sometimes he would make an effort to improve his conduct, particularly when he and his friends observed the twice-yearly custom of going to Holy Communion. 'The day previous to attending that ordinance, I used to refrain from doing certain things; and on the day itself I was serious, and also swore to God, with the emblem of the broken Body in my mouth, to become better, thinking that for that oath's sake I should be induced to reform. But after one or two days were over I was as bad as before.'

On his own confession, there was scarcely a sin which he did not commit during his school and college days, and his dissipations laid him low with illness, on one occasion for as long as three months. He was intelligent enough to realize that his profligate habits were going to endanger his career, and in consequence was often deeply depressed, lacking as he did the power to reform.

On one occasion, having got into debt, he tried a piece of successful but singularly unworthy subterfuge to obtain money. His father having sent him his usual allowance, he purposely showed this to some of his school-fellows. Then, having secretly broken open his trunk and guitar-case, he ran, in simulated panic, to inform the headmaster that he had been robbed, with the two forced locks to substantiate the story. Everyone sympathized, and friends rallied round and made up the money which he was supposed to have lost. Nevertheless, he paid bitterly in the end, because the headmaster, suspecting the truth, never really trusted him again, and he himself never afterwards felt comfortable in the presence of the headmaster's wife. She had looked after him with great kindness when he was ill, and now he had caused her trouble by creating an atmosphere of suspicion under her roof. Throughout those years, between the ages of fourteen and twenty, George Müller was haunted by a desire to change his worthless way of life for something better, but since he lacked the help of God, the pressure of the world was too strong for him.

When he was nineteen he left school and entered Halle University as a student of divinity. There were 1,260 students at Halle at that time, and no less than 900 of them were divinity students, with permission to preach in the Lutheran Church, the Established Church in Prussia, 'although' says Müller, 'I believe not nine of them feared the Lord.'

He now made strong resolutions to settle down to work, because he wanted to be chosen as pastor by some parish of repute. In Prussia at that time only the man with a good degree had any hope of obtaining one of the more valuable livings. His praiseworthy intentions came to nothing, however, and he was soon again frittering away his time with worthless companions. Spending money wildly, it was not long before he was pawning books and clothes, and borrowing from friends. He was worried and unhappy but as yet there was no sign of real repentance.

But like St. Francis, John Wesley, Lord Shaftesbury and others all down the ages, George Müller was undoubtedly a chosen vessel. Taken in isolation, any of the noteworthy events of his life during the next few years might be regarded as coincidences.

8

Viewed collectively, they appear as the hand of God leading him along a path undreamed-of at this time.

The first of these was his re-encounter, in a tavern, with Beta, a former school-fellow; a renewal of acquaintance which pleased them both. The friendship thus formed was a vital link in the chain of happenings that were to bring Müller to his life's work in Bristol, but oddly enough it came about through each misreading the other's motives, as they afterwards discovered. At school Beta had been religiously inclined, and in consequence too quiet and serious for young George's taste at that time. But since then he had become more careless. *He* now sought George Müller's company in the hope of being introduced into some gay society; Müller sought his because he thought that Beta would be a steady fellow who would help him to settle down. Only much later did either of them learn the other's true motive.

After an illness during the month of June, 1825, which he attributes to his own wrong-doing, Müller lived more moderately for a few weeks, chiefly from lack of means to do otherwise. But in August he and Beta, with two other friends, managed to scrape together enough money to indulge in the pastime of driving about the country for four days. This expensive little holiday merely whetted their appetites for more, and now at George's proposal, they formed the ambitious project of a trip to Switzerland. Such trifling obstacles as an entire absence of cash and no passports were soon got round by the resourceful George. Passports were obtained by forging letters from their parents, and money by pawning books and other articles.

The expedition took the form of a walking tour, and lasted forty-three days, the party getting as far as Mount Rigi. In later days Müller realized how providentially they had been preserved from illness and from getting separated from one another, which would have been disastrous, so short of funds and so far from home as they were.

He himself was treasurer for the party, and afterwards wrote, 'Oh, how wicked I was now!' when he recalled that he had contrived that his own expenditure should be only two-thirds of that of the rest. 'At last all of us became tired of seeing even the most beautiful views; and whilst at first, after seeing certain places, I had been saying with Horace, at the end of the day in my pagan heart, "*Vixi!* (I have lived)" I was now glad to get home again.'

He passed the remainder of that vacation at home, and with recourse as usual to many lies, he managed to satisfy his father as to how he had paid for his holiday abroad. He made good resolutions which were kept well enough during his three weeks at home, but which soon faded away on his return to Halle and his old companions.

But, he relates in his *Narrative*, the moment had come when God would have mercy upon him. 'Now, at a time when I was as careless about Him as ever, He sent His Spirit into my heart. I had no Bible, and had not read in it for years. I went to church but seldom; but, from custom, I took the Lord's Supper twice a year. I had never heard the Gospel preached up to the beginning of November, 1825. I had never met a person who told me that he meant, by the help of God, to live according to the Holy Scriptures. In short, I had not the least idea that there were any persons different from myself, except in degree.'

It was a Saturday afternoon, about the middle of November, 1825, when he was just two months past his twentieth birthday. Beta, with whom he had been for a walk, mentioned that he was in the habit of going on Saturday evenings to a meeting at the house of a Christian acquaintance. On further inquiry, he admitted that at the meeting they read the Bible, prayed and sang hymns, and a printed sermon was read. At once it seemed to George Müller that he had found something for which he had been seeking all his life. He pressed his friend to take him to the meeting, and, somewhat reluctantly, Beta consented. Beta could hardly be blamed for feeling that George would not like such a

11

way of spending an evening.

The meeting was held 'at the house of a believing tradesman of the name of Wagner'. On arrival Müller felt that he must apologize for coming uninvited, and never forgot the kind answer he received. 'Come as often as you please; house and heart are open to you.'

There was much that evening to leave on him a lasting impression. He saw what he had never seen before: someone *kneeling* to pray. One of the men present, who later was sent out to Africa by the London Missionary Society, knelt to ask a blessing on the meeting. He then read a chapter from the Bible, and a printed sermon. Germany at that time had not the religious freedom of England, and no regular meetings for explaining the Scriptures were permitted in Prussia unless an ordained minister were present. When the reading was finished a hymn was sung, and then prayers were led by the master of the house, Herr Wagner.

'Whilst he prayed,' says Müller, 'my feelings were something like this: "I could not pray as well, though I am much more learned than this illiterate man." The whole made a deep impression on me. I was happy; though if I had been asked why I was happy, I could not have explained it.'

As they were walking home, he said to Beta, 'All we have seen on our journey to Switzerland, and all our former pleasures, are as nothing in comparison with this evening.' He scarcely remembered afterwards what he did in getting back to his lodging, except that he lay peaceful and happy in bed. 'This shows that the Lord may begin His work in different ways. For I have not the least doubt that on that evening He began a work of grace in me, though I obtained joy without any deep sorrow of heart, and with scarcely any knowledge. That evening was the turning-point in my life. The next day, and Monday, and once or twice besides, I went again to the house of this brother; for it was too long to wait until Saturday came again.'

Eighty-seven years earlier John Wesley, too, according to his own account, had found Christ at a meeting in a private house late one evening. Wesley, like Müller, was a university man of great brilliance. Both were cool, clear-headed thinkers, with a superior intelligence which their tremendous faith and prolonged and concentrated prayers allowed the Holy Spirit to use to the uttermost. Both of them, right into old age, plunged into undertakings in the service of God which would appear to lesser men as impossible. But although their cases are thus far parallel, they are in other respects quite unlike. Wesley was thirty-four at the time of his conversion, and was already what, to the ordinary beholder, would seem to be a deeply religious man. George Müller was only twenty, and was practically a pagan and morally quite unstable. From that Saturday evening at Herr Wagner's house he became a Christian openly, but owns that he did not at once find the power to overcome his moral weaknesses. Some things he was able to put away at once; he kept away from bad company and ceased to frequent taverns. It was the subtler sins, such as telling lies, that clung to him for a time. He says, 'I no longer lived habitually in sin, though I was still often overcome, and sometimes even by open sins, though far less frequently than before, and not without sorrow of heart. I read the Scriptures, prayed often, loved the brethren, went to church from right motives, and stood on the side of Christ, though laughed at by my fellow students.' He finishes this part of his account of his early life by emphasizing that what his father's precepts had failed to do, what his own resolutions could not accomplish, he was thus at last able to do, constrained by the love of Jesus.

CHAPTER TWO

TO ENGLAND

The same energy which had in days gone by driven George Müller to get the most out of life in this world was now diverted to the service of God. It almost goes without saying that from the moment when he started to read missionary literature in the month of January, 1826, he felt stirred to become a missionary himself. But he was ever a man of deliberation rather than impulse. Self-restraint was one of his most marked characteristics. Only those who are prone to the upsurge of Good Ideas, and know the longing to put them into practice immediately, can fully appreciate the way in which he always subordinated such impulses to patient prayer for guidance. Throughout his life, for weeks, for months, sometimes for years, he would perseveringly pray for light on some project he had in mind, checking such guidance as he received by changing circumstances, and also by consultation with believing friends, until, sometimes quite suddenly, he would become certain that God was calling him to go forward with the scheme. Then he would begin to pray for the money to carry it out, with the absolute conviction that it would be supplied.

At this time he was still only twenty, and it is not surprising to learn that he fell in love with a girl he met at the Saturday meetings. He had reason to doubt that her parents would allow her to become the wife of a missionary, so he was soon in a state of conflict. Praying became difficult, and for some weeks he almost gave it

15

up. However, about Easter that year he became influenced by the example of Hermann Ball, a wealthy young man who had given up a life of ease to work among the Jews in Poland. Ball had renounced all he had for Christ's sake, while he himself had forsaken the Lord for a girl. 'The result of this comparison was that I was enabled to give up this connection, which I had entered into without prayer, and which had led me away from the Lord... I was, for the first time in my life, able to give myself up to Him.' The whole affair appears to have lasted only a few weeks, and probably the hearts of the two concerned were not deeply involved. It is evident that they were not meant for each other.

At last George Müller knew the joy of the wholly-dedicated Christian. He wrote to his father and brother to tell them of his newly-found happiness, and urged them by seeking the Lord to experience it for themselves. He was now to make the discovery, almost incredible to the eager youngster who has just given his allegiance to Christ, that friends and relatives seldom seem to find this a matter for rejoicing or even for approval. An angry answer was returned to his letter. Shortly afterwards he visited his father to get permission to offer for missionary service, for in Germany at that time parental consent was required before a young man could be accepted by a missionary society. Herr Müller, far from giving the requested consent, hurled reproaches at George. After all the money which he had expended on his education so that he might end his days in comfortable retirement in his son's parsonage, his plans were coming to nothing. He declared furiously that he would no longer consider George as his son. 'But the Lord gave me grace to remain steadfast. He then entreated me, and wept before me; but even this by far harder trial the Lord enabled me to bear.' Before leaving home again George spoke to his brother, reminding him of his own former dissolute life. He tried to show that, having been blessed by God, he could not do otherwise than live for Him now.

From that day forward he decided that he must support himself at the University, as it was unfair to take money from his father when he had no intention of following the career mapped out for him. Now he experienced for the first time what it was to live in dependence upon God for his daily needs, for soon after his return to Halle he obtained well-paid work teaching German to some American college professors, and translating lectures for them. For the first time in his life he had money enough and to spare. 'Thus,' he says, 'did the Lord richly make up to me the little I had relinquished for His sake.'

He was still wondering if he was called to be a missionary or not, and immature Christian that he was, had not enough patience to seek guidance through prayer. Instead, he took a step which, for such a purpose, seems strange to the modern Christian: he bought a ticket in a royal lottery, intending, if he won anything, to regard it as a sign that he was called to the mission field. He did win a small prize, offered himself to the Berlin Missionary Society, and was turned down because his father's consent was not forthcoming.

Years afterwards he recognized the mistake he had made, which was not so much his attempt to obtain speedy guidance in such a manner, as in thinking that anyone so ignorant and inexperienced in the Christian life could set up to be a teacher of others. He still knew so little about the most elementary truths of the Gospel that he would have had nothing to impart, and the impatience that drove him to force a decision by such a method would have been an insurmountable hindrance in so exacting a rôle as that of a missionary.

It would take up too much space to record all his gropings about for guidance during the next three years. He preached his first sermon in a village six miles from Halle on August 27th, 1826, at 8 o'clock in the morning at a chapel-of-ease, repeating it at 11 o'clock in the parish church. The sermon was one which he had committed to memory from some book, thinking, rightly, that he was too uninstructed to compose anything of the sort himself. It took him a week to learn and an hour to deliver. He says that he got no enjoyment from it, and it seems most unlikely that his hearers did either. In the afternoon, however, he thought that he would read the fifth chapter of St. Matthew's Gospel, and make such remarks upon it as occurred to him. The simple village folk listened to this with close attention, and he felt that they had understood it.

At about this time he lived for two months in the Orphan House built by the celebrated August Hermann Francke, Professor of Divinity at Halle in the early part of the eighteenth century. The Foundation included free lodging for poor students of divinity. Francke had built these houses at Halle in dependence upon God, and there can be little doubt that it was during George Müller's stay there that the seed of the idea was sown that was to come to fruit later in Bristol.

In the *Narrative*, Müller does not use the English term 'taking a degree', but as he states, writing of the year 1828, that he had completed his University course, and in the next paragraph says, 'as I had passed the University', presumably he was now a graduate. He was unusually gifted intellectually, being both a brilliant linguist (he refers somewhere to the fact that he spoke seven languages), and a fine mathematician. He kept the complicated accounts of his Institutions in Bristol so clearly and accurately that his system was employed by his successors for fifty years after his death.

Various circumstances combined to fill him with an urge to become a missionary to the Jews. He intensified his study of Hebrew, and applied to a society in London which existed to promote Christianity among the Jews. On June 13th, 1828, he received a letter stating that the Committee had agreed to take him as a student on six months' probation, provided that he would go to London. It seems to have been something of a struggle for him, a graduate, to agree to become a student again, but he thought it over calmly and resolved to submit. His father gave permission for him to go, and now the only obstacle in his way was conscription. Every Prussian male subject was obliged to serve a term in the army unless exempted by the King himself. This exemption was generally granted without difficulty to missionary candidates, but although several friends exerted their influence, it could not be obtained for Müller. Meanwhile several months went by, during which faith faltered to some extent. He also had serious stomach trouble, possibly an ulcer, and was very ill for several weeks, an illness no doubt brought on by the combination of conflict within his soul and worry caused by the uncertain state of his affairs. January, 1829, found him still without his passport to England, which could not be granted until he had either done his military service or got his exemption. It was an army major, a genuine Christian, who helped him to solve his difficulties. This officer suggested that his best course would be to offer himself at once for military service. He would then either have to enter the army immediately, or more probably be turned down on medical grounds. He took this advice, was fortunate enough to find the chief general and other senior officers concerned most sympathetic, both about his poor health and his desire to be a missionary, and obtained complete exemption for life from all military engagements.

He left home on February 10th, reached Rotterdam on February 22nd, and after a brief stay there, arrived in London on March 19th, 1829. He entered the seminary, and found himself bound to routine and regulations to an extent he had not known for many a year, so that he was tempted to throw up the idea of being a missionary to the Jews, and only the grace of God kept him steadfast. Most of his fellow-students were Germans with no university training, and had to study Latin, Greek, German, French and Hebrew. Müller, having a degree, was exempted from all except Hebrew. He records that he made little progress with English, living, as he was doing, among fellow-countrymen. Some months afterwards, when he was the only German in the midst of

English people, he soon became fluent, though in all his life he never quite lost his German accent.

His study of Hebrew was unremitting, and proved too much of a strain in his delicate state of health. On May 15th he fell ill again, and before long felt quite convinced that he was beyond recovery. But he was at peace with God. 'It was as if every sin of which I had been guilty was brought to my remembrance; but at the same time, I could realize that all my sins were completely forgiven; that I was washed and made clean, completely clean, in the blood of Jesus. The result of this was—great peace. I longed exceedingly to depart and be with Christ.'

When he had been ill for a fortnight, his doctor found him better, and soon his friends were urging him to go to the country for a change of air. Into such a low state had he fallen that he could hardly bear the thought of having again to face life in this world. It took a great effort of will to accept the fact that he must do so, and that his immediate duty was to journey to an unknown place and stay with strangers.

He went away for the change as planned by his friends, and this proved to be one of the most momentous steps he ever took. It was to Teignmouth in Devonshire that he went, and there he became acquainted with Henry Craik, soon to become his intimate friend and a little later his fellow-worker. The two men were of the same age, both highly intellectual, both constant in their study of the Bible. Craik was a distinguished classical scholar, and a graduate of St. Andrew's. One of his most marked characteristics was his humility, which made him refuse the doctorate offered him by his University and to recommend the name of another man. Years later the University offered it again, but he again declined. Yet he never lost his learning, and throughout his life studied the Scriptures daily in the original languages.

While in Teignmouth convalescing, George Müller attended the re-opening of a small meeting-house called Bethesda Chapel, and was much impressed by one of the speakers. Receiving an invitation to stay in Exmouth in the same house as this man, he accepted with alacrity and spent ten days there. It was during this period that he learnt to meditate on the Scriptures, and to rely upon them, as he had never done before. By the time that he returned to London he felt the change in his soul to be so great that it seemed like a second conversion.

He now began to gather with some of his fellow-students from six till eight each morning for prayer and Bible reading. So sweet did he find communion with God now that sometimes after communal prayers in the evening he would go to his room and pray until midnight. Then, so full of joy that he could not keep it to himself, he would go to the room of another student, and finding him in a similar state, pray with him until 1 a.m. or even 2 a.m. This would not prevent him from being up again at 6 a.m. to join the others in prayer. Such protracted prayer times seem to be characteristic of all great spiritual leaders. One feels for, and indeed is ready to echo the words of a young man, new in the faith, who on reading of the tremendous prayer sessions of such people as Müller and Wesley, exclaimed, 'But how on earth did they fill in the time?' The solution is presumably to be found in the quality of their prayers and meditations. Lesser folk at prayer lack the spiritual stamina and insight of great souls.

Müller now began to have serious doubts as to whether he ought to work for the Society, for various reasons which he sets forth in the *Narrative*. One of these was, that as the Society's missionary he would have to confine his ministrations to Jews, instead of preaching the Gospel to anyone as he might feel moved to do. But he naturally had scruples about cutting himself loose from the society which had provided his training. He pondered over this matter for many weeks, and eventually decided to offer to work for them for no salary, if they would allow him to travel freely about England, preaching both to Jews and to nominal Christians as the Spirit led him. Not unnaturally they were unable to accept him on such terms, but wrote back kindly to say that they would consider him again if in the future he should change his opinions. This never happened, and thus his connection with them was entirely dissolved. It must have seemed to the committee an unsatisfactory affair, and may even have made the members wonder if they had mistaken their own guidance in choosing a young man who had found himself unable to work for them after all. It is improbable that any among them had the power of seeing into the future, when George Müller's amazing spiritual gifts were to be such a witness to his own and subsequent generations of the faithfulness of God. He would probably never have come to England had The London Society for Promoting Christianity among the Jews not accepted him as a student. Had he remained with the Society he would never have settled in the West Country and embarked on his almost incredible career. The Society's part in the chain of circumstances was a dull but essential one.

★   ★   ★

Müller, who was in Devonshire at the time of his resignation from the Society, now settled down there, preaching in chapels in Exmouth, Teignmouth and Shaldon, laying stress on the

Second Coming and other doctrine that had impressed themselves so strongly upon him during his study of the Bible in recent months. Some of the people were greatly helped by his sermons, while others could not bear them. 'My preaching was also disliked there by many of the hearers,' is one of several similar naïve entries in his Journal.

Within a few weeks he received a definite invitation to become the minister at Ebenezer Chapel, Teignmouth, and although it had been his intention not to tie himself to any one place, but to become a travelling preacher, he felt that he was being guided to remain in Teignmouth for the time being. Finding that not quite all the members of the chapel wanted him for their minister, he would not accept any fixed salary at first, and for four months lived on the voluntary contributions of two members. 'After that time,' he says, 'the whole little church, eighteen in number, unanimously gave me an invitation to become their pastor.' They offered him £55 per annum, increasing the amount as the congregation grew.

During this year he became convinced of the necessity for Believers' Baptism, and although he had been christened in infancy, was baptized again. He also came to the conclusion, through his study of the Bible, that, though not obligatory, it was scriptural to receive the sacrament every Sunday.

CHAPTER THREE

TO BRISTOL

While still at the Seminary, Müller had heard a fellow-student speak of a certain Anthony Norris Groves, an Exeter dentist who had given up a practice bringing him in £1,500 a year to go out to Persia as a missionary, with his wife and children, trusting to God to supply all their needs. Now, only a few months later, Müller himself met the dentist's sister Mary.

It happened in this way. There was a Miss Paget in Exeter to whom Müller had been given a card of introduction. He called on her early in January, 1830, and she asked him to undertake a monthly preaching engagement at the village of Poltimore, just outside Exeter. He agreed to do this, and as he would now need somewhere to stay each time he came to Exeter, Miss Paget recommended him to lodge with the Hakes who kept a boarding-school for young children at Northernhay House. Mrs. Hake being an invalid, Mary Groves, then a woman of twenty-nine, was keeping house for her.

George Müller, only twenty-four but obviously of a mature outlook, had been coming to the conclusion that it would be better for a young man in his position to be married. Now, regularly meeting with Mary Groves, he was greatly attracted to her. Only one consideration kept him back, and that was the thought that he would be doing his friends the Hakes an unkind turn if he took away their valuable assistant while Mrs. Hake was incapacitated. In great conflict of mind, he prayed long and earnestly before he could come to a decision. What finally removed any lingering scruples was the realization that Mary was as much in love with him as he was with her. Praying that someone suitable might be found to replace her, he wrote, on August 15th, asking her to be his wife, and when he went to Exeter four days later, she accepted him. Their first action together, which typically foreshadowed the whole of their married life, was to fall on their knees and ask God to bless their intended union.

In the following October, another housekeeper having been found for Mrs. Hake, they were married. The wedding was of the simplest nature. They walked to the church, which was St. David's, Exeter, Northernhay House (demolished in 1913) being in that parish. The following is a verbatim copy of the entry in the register.

George Miller, of the Parish of East Teignmouth, in the County of Devon, Minister of the Gospel, Bachelor, and Mary

Groves, of this Parish, Spinster, were married in this church by Banns this 7th day of October, 1830

By me, John Abbott, Incumbent.

This marriage was solemnized between us

George Miller
Mary Groves

In the Presence of

W. Hake
Maria Kennaway
Arthur Groves

Notice that George Müller signs himself as 'Miller'. He really preferred to be addressed by the anglicized form of his name, probably because 'Miller' is nearer to the German pronunciation of 'Müller' than is 'Muller', as it is often rendered. He does not, however, seem to have persisted with the English spelling, as his signature later in life appears simply as 'George Müller'. He became a naturalized Englishman on December 18th, 1861.

After the ceremony at the church, the newly-married pair and their friends returned to Northernhay House. Müller himself describes what followed in these words: 'We ... had no wedding breakfast, but in the afternoon had a meeting of Christian friends in Mr. Hake's house, and commemorated the Lord's death; and then I drove off in the stage-coach with my beloved bride to Teignmouth, and next day we went to work for the Lord.'

In his *Narrative* he thus records his marriage:

'On October 7th, 1830, I was united by marriage to Miss Mary Groves, sister of the brother whose name has been mentioned. This step was taken after prayer and deliberation, from a full conviction that it was better for me to be married; and I have never regretted since, either the step itself, or the choice, but desire to be truly grateful to God for giving me such a wife.'

It does not sound romantic, put like that, but actually it was the perfect marriage. She was one with him in outlook and conviction. After her death he could say, 'Our happiness in God, and in each other, was indescribable. We had not some happy days every year, nor a month of happiness a year; but we had twelve months of happiness every year, and thus year after year. Often and often did I say to that beloved one, and this again and again even in the fortieth year of our conjugal union—"My darling, do you think there is a couple in Bristol, or in the world, happier than we are ?"'

Just three weeks after their wedding, the newly-married pair, believing as they did so literally in the promises of the Bible, took that step of faith with which the name of George Müller has ever since been associated: they decided to depend on God alone for the supply of all their needs. His salary being made up by pew rents, Müller felt led to relinquish it completely. Wishing that all contributions to his support might be made spontaneously, he asked that these should be put in a box in the chapel. He resolved that from that time forward he would ask no fellow-creature to aid him financially, but make his requests to God only. Also, he determined to run into no debt, however small, but to pay for everything that he and his wife needed at the time of obtaining it. They lived ever afterwards on this plan, and never went hungry, although their faith was tried to the utmost. Sometimes during that first year they sat down to a meal with their last loaf on the table, and not a penny in the house towards the next one. Either money, or occasionally contributions in kind, arrived in time for the next meal.

The Müllers carried this principle of mentioning their wants only to God to the extent of making no definite answer to inquiries as to whether or not they were in need of money at any particular moment. On November 30th, 1830, Müller records in his diary, 'Our money was reduced to about eight shillings. When I was praying with my wife this morning, the Lord brought to my mind the state of our purse, and I was led to ask him for some money. About four hours after, we were with a sister at Bishopsteighton, and she said to me, "Do you want any money?" I said, "I told the brethren, dear sister, when I gave up my salary, that I would for the future tell the Lord *only* about my wants." She replied, "But He has told me to give you some money. About a fortnight ago I asked Him what I should do for Him, and He told me to give you some money, and last Saturday it came again so powerfully to my mind, and has not left me since, and I felt it so forcibly last night that I could not help speaking of it to brother P." My heart rejoiced, seeing the Lord's faithfulness, but I thought it better not to tell her about our circumstances, lest she should be influenced to give accordingly; and I was also assured that, if it were of the Lord, she could not but give. I therefore turned the conversation to other subjects, but when I left she gave me two guineas. We were full of joy on account of the goodness of the Lord.'

This occurred again and again throughout his life, both as regards his private income, and of the funds for his vast projects for the orphans and for missionary work. However urgent was the need for money, and though he might have prayed for days on end without any apparent answer to his prayers, though the next meal for himself and those dependent on him was not yet in sight, he would never tell anyone, man or woman, however they framed their question, that he was in desperate need of supplies. Instead he renewed his prayers to his Heavenly

Father, and either money or food always came in time to save the situation.

He and his wife did not unlock the box in the chapel into which were put the offerings for their support. Other members undertook to do this and hand the money over to them. When this plan was originated, Müller had asked that the box might be opened once a week, but for some reason or other those in charge of it were not at all punctual in carrying out this duty, and often the box would remain unopened for anything up to five weeks. Naturally this caused great inconvenience to the Müllers, but they would not press for the money to be passed over, however badly they might be needing it. Müller felt that if he repeated his request for a weekly settlement it would hinder the testimony he wished to make to the faithfulness of God. So when there was a delay, he would pray that God would put it into the hearts of his friends to do as they had promised. It must have called for uncommon self-restraint on the part of husband and wife when, for instance, they found themselves very short of money on January 28th, and yet had seen, on January 24th, someone opening the box, who was so dilatory as not to have passed over the money four days later. But they made it again a matter for prayer, and within a short time the contents of the box, £1 8s. 1d., was handed over to them.

Repeatedly during that first year of married life the Müllers were down to their last halfpenny, but they went on in faith, paying ready money for everything they bought, and never actually coming to want. At the end of 1831 their accounts showed that they had been sent, in answer to their prayers, the sum of £131 18s. 8d., and gifts in kind worth at least twenty pounds. Müller writes: 'Had I had my regular salary, humanly speaking I should not have had nearly so much; but whether this would have been the case or not, this is plain, that I have not served a hard Master, and that is what I delight to show.'

On February 19th, 1832, he records an instance of healing by faith. On the previous day he had suffered a haemorrhage, almost certainly due to a gastric ulcer; the same trouble had befallen him five years before in Halle, on which occasion he had been ill for weeks. This time his friends expected him to be completely incapacitated, and on the 19th, which was Sunday, they called at his house to make arrangements with him for others to take over his three preaching engagements for that day. He asked them to call again in an hour for his answer. After they had left, he felt that God was giving him faith to get up and dress. He reached the chapel with difficulty, as he was very weak, but was able to preach with as strong a voice as usual. After the meeting one of his friends who

34

was a doctor urged him not to attempt to address the afternoon meeting for fear of injuring himself. His reply was that he would indeed consider it great presumption to do so had not the Lord given him faith. He preached both in the afternoon and evening, and felt stronger after each meeting, which he took as a proof that God was with him. Within four days he was as well as ever. This is perhaps a fitting place in which to stress that George Müller's character can only be comprehended if we take his utterances literally as he himself took the promises of the Bible. If we write off his comments as pious platitudes, the events and still more the achievements of his life will be unexplained, and the man himself will remain an enigma. His own explanations of his experiences are the only ones which are credible. In the present case, for instance, he adds to his account of his healing a warning to the readers of his *Narrative*, which clearly shows that it was not obstinacy in the face of medical advice which prompted him to act as he did, nor was it the mere exercise of will-power, but a simple work of faith that wrought his cure. To quote his own words: 'I would earnestly warn everyone who may read this not to imitate me if he has no faith; but if he has, it will, as good coin, most assuredly be honoured by God. I could not say that if such a thing happened again, I would act in the same way;

for when I have not been nearly so weak as when I broke the blood-vessel, having no faith, I did not preach; yet if it were to please the Lord to give me faith, I might be able to do the same, though even weaker than at the time spoken of.'

In the spring of the year 1832 he began to feel that Teignmouth was no longer for him, and that he must soon leave it. Henry Craik had gone to Bristol on a month's visit, and Müller felt in his own mind that Craik would remain there, returning to Teignmouth only to take leave of his friends, and this proved to be the case. Craik wrote to urge his friend to come to Bristol. Müller decided to go there for a short stay, but felt inwardly inclined towards Torquay, to preach there a few times and then travel further. He prayed for guidance, but his path did not become clear to him for some time.

One entry in his journal, quoted in the *Narrative*, shows that he was far from robust as a young man, and that he tired easily. It also reveals that to him, as to others less strong in faith, bodily fatigue was an almost insurmountable hindrance to prayer.

'I left this morning for Bristol. I preached with little power (as to my own feeling) in Exeter, from three to half-past four. At five I left for Taleford, where I preached in the evening, likewise with little power. I was very tired in body, and had therefore little prayer.

But still, in both places, the believers seemed refreshed ... I went to bed at eleven, very, very tired.' It is not clear whether the hour and a half's preaching at Exeter was inclusive of the rest of the service, or not; if not, one suspects that the preacher was not the only one suffering from fatigue by the end! It was, of course, still the day of lengthy sermons such as no modern congregation could endure. Later in his life, at all events, he was not so long-winded. Mrs. Rendle-Short told me that in her youth she and the other children of the family were always glad when Mr. Müller was to preach; he could be relied upon to close the meeting punctually.

On April 22nd he preached his first sermons in Bristol, at Gideon and Pithay chapels. He was impressed with the feeling that he was being called to Bristol, but both he and Henry Craik decided that they must go back to Teignmouth first, where, in familiar surroundings, and uninfluenced by anyone in Bristol, they might quietly wait upon God and be led to the right conclusion. Nevertheless, before leaving Bristol they felt nearly certain that they were meant to work there, though they did not yet see in what circumstances. Then a friend offered to hire Bethesda Chapel, and himself be responsible for the rent for one year, on the understanding that if the nucleus of a congregation were gathered together, its members should help him to pay the rent.

Müller explains that this was the only way in which they could take the chapel, as it was their rule never to run into debt. He and Craik agreed to undertake the ministry at Bethesda, but not in any fixed capacity. They wanted to be free to preach as they felt guided, without being bound by any stipulations. They also insisted that pew rents should be abolished, and that they should continue to live, in regard to the supply of their material needs, as they had done in Devonshire. Most of this was arranged by correspondence while they were in Teignmouth taking leave of the people there, and on May 25th, 1832, they arrived back in Bristol to settle there permanently. So began George Müller's long association with Bethesda Chapel in Great George Street, Bristol, where it stood almost opposite the gates of another famous institution, St. Brandon's, the Clergy Daughters' School. After his death the chapel remained there for another forty-three years, and then, on a night in 1941, during the blitz on Bristol, it was completely burnt out. Not a trace of it remains, and grass now covers the land on which it stood. The building which one German had helped to make into a meeting-place for believers during a ministry of more than sixty years, was in one brief hour destroyed by the act of an unknown fellow-countryman. But Müller would have been the first to point out that the value of a house of prayer lies not in the building itself, but in the seed sown in the hearts of those who have worshipped there.

An incident is recorded in the *Autobiography* which shows how, where people are praying, the most trivial motives may lead a soul to its blessing. A girl came to Bethesda merely out of curiosity to hear Müller's foreign accent, as some words had been mentioned to her which he did not pronounce correctly. No sooner had she entered the chapel than she saw herself as a sinner. She had meant to stay for only a few minutes, but felt riveted to her seat while he was speaking, and she remained to the end of the meeting. From that moment her heart was changed, and she became a genuine believer.

In July that same year, Bristol was visited by cholera, which made fearful ravages. 'We have reason to believe that great numbers die daily in this city. Who may be the next, God alone knows. I have never realized before so much the nearness of death... Just now, ten in the evening, the funeral bell is ringing, and has been ringing the greater part of this evening. It rings almost all day.' It is hard for us nowadays to realize just how terrible those epidemics of cholera were. Only too often, the victims were ill for a few hours, and all was over. Müller records that, with one exception, none of the Christian people among whom he and Craik worked were taken ill. The two men visited many cholera patients by day and by night, but they and their families were all preserved.

On September 17th, 1832, the Müllers' first child was born; a daughter, whom they called Lydia.

CHAPTER FOUR

THE SCRIPTURAL KNOWLEDGE INSTITUTION

February 25th, 1834. George Müller wrote in his diary: 'I was led again this day to pray about forming a new Missionary Institution, and felt still more confirmed that we should do so. The Institution will be called "The Scriptural Knowledge Institution for Home and Abroad".'

So began one of the great projects to which his life would henceforth be devoted; or rather, since the one sole object of his devotion was God Himself, and his chief aim to glorify God before men, it would be truer to say, one of the means through which he sought to achieve this aim.

This society, with its unwieldy title, typical of the early nineteenth century, is still active today. It started with four distinct purposes, which are always referred to in the *Reports* and elsewhere as the First Four Objects, to distinguish them from Müller's other great project, the Orphan Houses. The Four Objects were:

1. To assist Sunday Schools, Day Schools and Adult Schools, and where possible to start new ones. The teachers in all these schools had to be professing Christians of Evangelical outlook, and of course the Bible teaching was what would nowadays be termed Fundamentalist.

2. To sell Bibles and Testaments to the poor at low prices, and if necessary, to give them free of cost.

3. To aid missionary effort. This did not mean that the Institution was a missionary society in the ordinary sense, nor did it make grants to any particular societies. Financial aid was sent from time to time to individual freelance missionaries to help and encourage them in their lonely task.

4. To circulate tracts in English and in various foreign languages. The centre which George Müller founded and developed for the production and distribution of these tracts, Scripture portions, and so on, has now become a handsome bookshop in Park Street, Bristol, known as the Evangelical Christian Literature Bookshop.

So much for the Objects for which the

41

Institution was founded. Not less important were the rules which Müller and his friends laid upon themselves concerning its funds. Briefly, these were as follows:

1. They considered every Christian to be bound, in one way or another, to help the cause of Christ.
2. They decided not to ask unconverted people of rank or wealth to be the Institution's patrons, as that would dishonour God.
3. They would not actually ask money from those who made no Christian profession, but if such people should offer it of their own accord, they would feel free to accept it.
4. They would not invite non-Christians to take part in managing the affairs of the Institution.
5. They would not contract debts, but would act according to the funds at their disposal, which they would seek for by secret prayer to God.
6. They would not reckon the success of the Institution by statistics, but by God's blessing on the work, which they expected to be in proportion to the extent in which they waited upon Him in prayer.
7. They wished to maintain the Institution in simple accordance with Scripture,

avoiding any needless singularity which might make them conspicuous, and thankfully receiving any advice which experienced Christians might have to offer.

The Orphan House, when it came to be founded, was a fifth Object of the Institution, but while the Orphan Houses are well known, probably the other Four Objects are less so, and to most people the name of George Müller stands for the founder of an orphanage, and they never think of him in any other connection. Far larger sums of money were contributed for the Orphan Houses than for the other objects, no doubt because the needs of the Orphans appealed even to those who might not perhaps have entirely agreed with Müller and his associates on every point of doctrine. People of different outlook may all read the Bible with a most earnest desire to find the truth, and yet the conclusions they draw from it, and the interpretation they put upon what they read, will not be the same. Individuals differ so much in mental capacity, temperament and natural and spiritual gifts, and grow up in such diverse environments with such inequality of opportunity; no one human being can perceive the whole of the Almighty God. It was given to George Müller to see Him as the One who hears and answers prayer, and he demonstrated this truth about the nature of God as few mortals have ever done.

Though the religious outlook that governed the application of the first four Objects might make them rather lacking in appeal to minds cast in a different mould, it was plain that they were very dear to the heart of Müller himself. The Scriptural Knowledge Institution, in spite of its heavy title, must over the years have done much to help forward the Kingdom of God, and to encourage missionaries battling against great odds in hostile surroundings. Those Day and Sunday Schools must have turned out many genuine Christians, as well as good citizens. The very large circulation of low-priced Bibles and other literature must have met the deep need of thousands of the under-privileged in many countries, and this work still goes on.

On March 19th, 1834, Mary Müller gave birth to her second child, a son. During the two years that the Müllers and the Craiks had lived in Bristol, they had shared a house. Now that there were three children and two sets of parents in a house with only six rooms, it became necessary to separate. On May 4th the Müllers moved to another address.

At the beginning of 1835, Anthony Norris Groves, Müller's brother-in-law, arrived in England on his way to Germany to recruit missionaries for the East Indies. Groves asked Müller to accompany him as interpreter, and to help in choosing the right men. Now, as at several other times in his life, George Müller experienced the longing to become a foreign missionary himself, but to him the stirring up of enthusiasm was not to be confused with guidance. He prayed constantly about it, but could never feel that God was calling him to go overseas. It was not until late in life, after forty years of quite different work in Bristol, that he actually did go on missionary tours in distant lands.

But Groves's proposal did seem to him to be his concern, and he agreed to go. He and Groves left London on March 6th. The length of time which it took them to reach their destination, and the primitive conveyances in which they travelled, bring home to one how early it still was in the century. The steam train had only just been invented, and hardly any lines had yet been laid; Queen Victoria was not yet on the throne. The travellers arrived in Dover on the morning of the 7th, and the next day being a Sunday, Müller preached twice in a local chapel. On the 9th the sea was too rough for the packet boat to sail according to schedule, but on the following day the crossing was made, after which the journey as far as Paris was made by stage-coach. On the 15th Müller and his companion set off for Strasbourg, travelling in a vehicle known as the Malle Post. In the *Narrative* Müller wrote:

45

'This quickest of all conveyances in France carries only two passengers, and we were thus able freely to converse and pray together, which was refreshing indeed.' But what a tiring journey! 'From six o'clock in the evening of the 15th, until this afternoon at half-past-one, when we arrived in Strasbourg, we were continually shut up in the Malle Post, with the exception of yesterday morning about seven, and last night about eleven, when we were allowed half an hour for our meals.' Then he adds, 'Though we had travelled forty-four hours, yet as soon as we had finished our business at Strasbourg we left this evening for Basle, trusting in the Lord for strength for the third night's travelling.'

He went to several places in Germany, and on March 30th reached Halle. Of the journey there he records that at one point he found himself alone in the coach, which gave him opportunity to pray audibly for about an hour 'which strengthened and refreshed my soul. It was particularly kind of the Lord to give me an opportunity of praying aloud, as, on account of having travelled forty-eight hours uninterruptedly, my body was too tired to allow me to continue for any length of time in mental prayer.' It is encouraging to weaker mortals who find concentration difficult that even George Müller could not pray silently when he was fatigued.

Halle was the place where, nearly ten years

before, he had found God, and he records that, tired though he was, his heart was too full to allow him to sleep. First he visited the house where he had been converted, and then went to call on Professor Tholuck, Councillor of the Consistory, who had been his tutor and who was a true Christian man. He and his former pupil held slightly divergent religious opinions, but that did not prevent him from receiving him most kindly. Müller wrote, 'He made me lodge with him, and gave thereby a testimony that differences of views, concerning certain parts of God's truth, ought not to separate the children of God.'

He spent the next few weeks in revisiting the scenes of former days, and renewing old friendships. On April 4th he arrived at Heimersleben, where his father still lived. 'At last I arrived at my father's house. How affecting to meet him once more!'

He stayed there for five days, longing for his father's conversion, and yet diffident of too direct an approach. He set himself to show every possible kindness and attention to the old man, and twice was given the chance to witness for Christ to his family. 'This afternoon a friend of my father's called—one who knows not the Lord. After a few minutes the Lord gave me opportunity of setting before him the fundamental truths of the Gospel, and the joy and comfort they afford, and have afforded to *me*. Thus a way was opened to me of stating the truth more fully than ever I had been able to do before by words of mouth in the presence of my father and brother, without saying to them, "Thou art the man."' Also, one evening was spent in relating to them how God had dealt with him in England, and supplied his needs in answer to prayer. Both father and brother seemed to feel, at least for the moment, the blessedness of such a life. Before George Müller left Heimersleben his father said to him, 'May God help me to follow your example, and to act according to what you have said to me.'

On April 8th father and son drove together to Halberstadt, where they parted, the old man in tears. George was alone in the mail coach, and it was to him a solemn experience, as he drove along, to be covering the ground so familiar to him during his former dissolute life. On the road from Brunswick to Celle he was unable to avoid overhearing what he describes as 'a most fearfully wicked, profligate, infidel and scoffing conversation between the conductor and a student;' and self-contemptuously he adds, 'the only testimony I gave was—complete silence all the time.' He spent an unhappy day in Celle, waiting for the Hamburg coach to leave at four in the afternoon. 'It has been far from well with me in my soul today. That awful conversation has been spiritual poison to me.' He reached Bristol again on April 15th.

On June 22nd, his father-in-law passed away. It was a sad time for the Müllers. Both children were ill, and on June 25th fifteen-months-old Elijah died of pneumonia. Towards the end, Müller no longer prayed for the child's recovery, but that his wife might be supported under the trial if the little boy were taken, and that the end might come speedily to spare the child further suffering. Both of these prayers were granted. It may seem strange that George Müller, of all people, whose prayers had so often prevailed, should have ceased so soon to ask for his son's life to be spared, for his wife's sake if not for his own. But to him there were always two parts to a prayer: the discerning of God's will and the actual making of the request. It may be that he intuitively sensed that the child's brief earthly course was run. One fact only is sure; he, and possibly his wife also, ceased to petition God for their little son's life, and Elijah died. Only their little daughter Lydia was left, and she grew up to be a blessing to her parents, a true Christian, and by all accounts a very sweet person.

Both Müller and his friend Craik seem to have had poor health as young men, and they were both ill during the summer of 1835. In August, Müller became too poorly to stay at work. A holiday seemed imperative, but funds were low. However, on each of the three dates, August 26th, August 29th and August 30th, five pounds was given him for the express purpose of getting a change of air. On September 2nd he, with his wife, child and their servant, went to Portishead. May one be pardoned a pang of envy! Imagine the sum of £15 and only two days notice being all that was needed to transport a family to the seaside, there to accommodate them for a restful holiday! But perhaps one's envy is misplaced in this instance. Poor George Müller did not enjoy himself there at all. He was in a state of depression. In addition he had the vexation of having to live a life which he describes as a great trial to him. He heartily disliked being obliged to take so much care of himself physically, and having as his chief occupations eating and drinking, walking, bathing, and—that favourite of nineteenth century doctors' orders—horse exercise. He longed to be back at work in Bristol. However, he was the most conscientious man alive, and he persevered with the regime. This suffered a sharp set-back when he discovered that the man from whom he was hiring his horse had no licence. He felt himself bound, as a believer, to act according to the laws of the country, so could hire the horse no longer, and no other was available in the place. 'As horse exercise seems the most important, humanly speaking, for my restoration, and as this seems the only horse to be had, we came to the conclusion to leave Portishead tomorrow.' Immediately afterwards he received an invitation to stay with friends in the Isle of Wight, and only lack of enough money hindered the family from starting off. This obstacle was removed by the arrival next day of the sum of £6 13s., which was owing to them, and another letter containing a gift of £2. They reached the Isle of Wight on September 19th.

On October 9th he spent the day weighing the pros and cons of publishing what later became known as *The Narrative of the Lord's dealing with George Müller*. He had for some time thought of giving in print some account of God's goodness to him, for the encouragement of others. While in the Isle of Wight he read the life of John Newton, which impelled him to put his notion into practice. During the next eighteen months he worked intermittently at what subsequently became the first volume of the *Narrative*.

CHAPTER FIVE

THE FIRST ORPHAN HOUSES

George Müller had for a long time been turning over in his mind the plan of starting an orphanage to be run in utter dependence upon God for all supplies. He was, of course, familiar with the story of the great A. H. Francke, in whose Orphan Houses in Halle he himself had lodged for several weeks in 1826. On November 20th, 1835, when he was just thirty, he went to tea at a friend's house, and there found a biography of Francke. This may seem a trivial incident, hardly worth recording, yet it is noteworthy, because it seems to have moved him to turn thought into action, and to take practical steps about his orphanage project.

As always with him, his first move in the matter was to pray. He did not as yet pray for the money which would be needed, but that God would guide him. He entreated God, if the project was not in accordance with His Will, to take every thought concerning it from his mind. Also, he searched his heart to discover his own motives. The result was an increasing conviction that he should go forward with the scheme.

By way of further guidance, he sought the advice of a close friend, John Corser. Corser, a Church of England clergyman, had resigned his living to work as a City Missionary in Bristol and to help George Müller. He took an encouraging view of the plan, so Müller had posters printed to announce a public meeting on December 9th.

Four days before that date, while reading the eighty-first Psalm, Müller was struck by the tenth verse: 'Open thy mouth wide, and I will fill it.' For the first time he felt impelled to pray for the means for his projected Orphan House. Falling on his knees, he asked his heavenly Father for premises, for one thousand pounds, and for the right people to care for the children. Two days later came the first answer to his prayer: the sum of one shilling, the first tiny fraction of close on a million pounds which was to flow in for the orphans during his lifetime.

The 9th of December found him in a state of depression about the project. 'But,' he says, 'as soon as I began to speak at the meeting, I received peculiar assistance from God, felt great peace and joy, and assurance that the work is of God.' There was no collection at the meeting, and no speaker other than himself, as he wished to avoid working upon anybody's feelings. However, someone handed ten shillings, and a Christian woman offered herself for the work.

It was a particularly striking venture of faith on the part of Müller and his associates, as they were at that time rather short of funds for the other four Objects of the Scriptural Knowledge Institution, and they would never contract debts. Müller and Corser gave themselves to prayer almost without remission for five whole days, after which their prayers began to be answered, and within a few days fifty pounds had come in.

It did not seem necessary for the Orphan House to be endowed, or even for there to be the promise of annual subscriptions. They asked simply that they might have the money to rent a house, and to furnish and otherwise equip it. 'We trust to be enabled by the Lord, who has taught us to ask for our daily bread, to look to Him for the supply of the daily wants of those children whom He may be pleased to put under our care.'

Their only other urgent request was for suitable people to work with the children. They had already determined to engage as masters, mistresses and matrons only those whom they knew to be true believers, and who were in other respects qualified for the work. This principle has been followed throughout the history of the Orphan Houses. It is not impossible that a hypocrite may occasionally have gained a place on the staff, but even if not soon dismissed, it seems unlikely that such a person could have elected to stay for more than a brief period. Only individuals who were themselves of a very real faith could wish to work in an institution where not only salaries, but the prompt arrival of meals, depended on timely answers to prayer. Many and many a time over the years everyone on the staff knew that not only did there appear to be no prospect, humanly speaking, of their wages ever being paid again, but that there was nothing in the house for next day's meals. Nevertheless, they did not panic, but courageously joined their leader in yet more prayer. George Müller was not the only one who demonstrated faith to a heroic degree. Those other names, unlike his, may not be remembered on earth, but surely they are written in heaven. The two applicants who wrote as follows are probably typical of many during the ensuing century: 'We propose ourselves for the service of the intended Orphan House, if you think us qualified for it; also to give up all the furniture, etc, which the Lord has given us, for its use; and to do this without receiving any salary whatever; believing that if it is the will of the Lord to employ us, He will supply all our need.'

Very early in his *Narrative* Müller stressed his reasons for wishing to found the Orphan House. He admits that he certainly did wish to provide orphaned children with the physical care they needed, and to have them taught and trained to take their places in this world. He also longed to be used in training their souls for God's service. These were to him very genuine motives for providing an orphanage, which was desperately needed at that period, when early death overtook so many, and large families bereaved of both parents were a commonplace. Some parentless children were left to the tender mercies of relatives who unwillingly took them into their own overcrowded households. Others went to the workhouse; many lived as homeless waifs on the streets. Dr. Barnardo was not to begin his great work for another thirty years, nor the Waifs and Strays' Society to function for another fifty. Müller tells how moved he had been, while living in Teignmouth, by the sight of so many ragged and wretched children running wild in the streets.

Nevertheless, these considerations were but secondary. His paramount aim was, to have something to point to as a visible proof that God hears and answers prayer. He describes how he was constantly in contact with earnest Christian people who yet lacked the faith to trust God utterly, and who worried about the approach of old age, with the fear of being driven through sheer poverty to the workhouse. He would try to convince such people that God never fails those who trust in Him, but he could see that they were thinking, though they might not actually say so, that times have changed, and that what might once have been true no longer held good. They could not grasp that God is the Living God, who never changes. Müller was saddened in spirit when he encountered this attitude, as he so often did, but realized that no argument of his would alter it. He longed to show, by visible proof, that God is willing and able, at the present day, to help those who rely upon Him. This was his most compelling motive for establishing the Orphan House: to provide, by its means, just such a proof.

The day which had been fixed for making

applications for the reception of orphan children came and went without a single one having been sent in. This brought home to Müller the discomforting realization that he had prayed in connection with the Orphan Houses for everything except the children who were to fill it. He had taken it for granted that there would be plenty of applications. This disturbed him very much. He had all along harboured misgivings that he might, after all, be going contrary to God's will by starting this new work, and this seemed to show further grounds for them. He spent the whole of the evening of February 3rd, 1836, in humble prayer, examining his motives once more. But at the end of all his heart-searching it still seemed to him that if the Orphan House were established and were to prosper, that more than anything would tend to the glory of God. At last he felt at peace, and could pray with all his heart that orphans would be brought for admission. The very next day an application was received, and by May 18th, less than four months later, forty-two had been made.

For the first Orphan House, Müller rented that in which he himself had been living: Number 6, Wilson Street. The rent was low, and being a large house, it seemed suitable. He and his friends furnished and equipped it for thirty children, and on April 11th began to take them in. The children in this first house were girls between seven and twelve years old.

Within a very short time plans were having to be made to open a second Orphan House, this time for little children from babyhood to seven years. Already several applications for infants had been received. Müller found, also in Wilson Street, an excellent house for the Infants, which he says could hardly have been more suitable had it been built for the purpose, but the opening of the Infant Orphan House was delayed, though money was available to start it, because for some time a suitable matron could not be found. He was always exceedingly careful as to whom he engaged to work in the Orphan Houses, and of course it was important to find a woman who, besides being a genuine Christian, was capable, reliable and kind. However, someone suitable must have been discovered, because by November 28th, 1836, all was in order, and the House was opened.

Only ten months later he started a third House, this time for boys over seven. The need for one was pressing, partly because there was so little provision for orphan boys in Bristol, and partly because there was no other way to provide for the boys from the Infant House when they reached the age of seven. In these days, boys and girls in Children's Homes often live together in the same house like the members of a family, but at that period complete segregation of the sexes was the rule in schools for all classes of society.

Before embarking upon the establishment of this third House George Müller decided that three conditions must be fulfilled. Someone must come forward to assist him as steward, taking over such work as the keeping of the accounts and dealing with the ordinary business connected with running the orphanage. He needed, too, to find a genuine Christian to be master of the boys, and also other staff to look after them. Finally, he resolved that until he had a sum large enough to furnish a house for the boys, to clothe them and to leave a little over to begin running the house, he could not feel that it was God's will to enlarge the field of work in this way. In due course these needs were all met, and the Boys' Orphan House was in full occupation, in the same street as the two others.

During the months of May and June, 1836, Müller was confined to the house with some ailment which prevented his getting about without making him too ill to work. This proved a blessing in disguise, as it gave him the chance he needed to concentrate on writing his *Narrative* for the press. He had started it earlier, but with so much to engage his attention it had had to be laid aside. Now, however, his enforced leisure enabled him to complete more than half the manuscript, and by May, 1837 it was almost ready for publication.

Now he gave himself with renewed intensity to prayer for the balance of the thousand pounds for which he had first prayed on December 2nd, 1835.

'I earnestly desired that the book might not leave the press before every shilling of that sum had been given, in answer to prayer, without one single individual having been asked by me for anything, that I might have the sweet privilege of bearing testimony to God in this book.'

On June 16th he joyfully records that the whole thousand pounds is made up, the £55 10s. 0d. which was still lacking having come in through four different contributions. 'To the glory of God, whose I am, and whom I serve, I would state that every shilling of this money, and all the articles of clothing and furniture, which have been mentioned in the foregoing pages, have been given me without one single individual having been asked by me for anything. As the Lord has condescended most fully, and above my expectations, to answer my prayers, will you help me, brethren and sisters, beloved in the Lord, to praise Him for His condescension. It is a wonderful thing that such a worthless, faithless servant as I am, should have power with God. Take courage from this for yourselves, brethren. Surely, if such a one as I am, so little conformed to the mind of Jesus, has his prayers answered, may not you also, at last, have your requests granted to you.' He concludes by saying that at the time of writing he is waiting on the Lord for £17 10s., the rent for two schoolrooms (no doubt he refers to two of the Day Schools), and deplores the fact that though he believes that God is willing to send it, still he does not feel as sure of being able to pay this rent as he would if he had the money already in his pocket. Only absolute faith in God was good enough, and when he failed in this even temporarily, he felt that he was not giving Him the glory due to Him.

The *Narrative* is extremely lucid, showing a mastery of English grammar and syntax that only a talented linguist could have acquired in so short a time. But Müller's style is old-fashioned to the modern reader, and many of his phrases have a scriptural flavour that is due, no doubt, to his constant reading of the Bible to the exclusion of almost everything else. Such a manner of writing tends to convey the impression that the writer is inclined to self-complacency. The interjection of such expressions as 'Such a wretch as I' used, as they certainly were in Müller's case, with complete sincerity, will not be enough to remove such a suspicion from the incredulously-minded. But such an entry as the following, though it contains no conscious expression of humility, nevertheless breathes spontaneously its true spirit. 'August 15th, 1837. Today the first 500 copies of the first part of my *Narrative* arrived, and I had, once more, some conflict of mind whether, after all, I had not been mistaken in this matter. A sort of trembling came over me, and a wish to retrace the step. Judging, however, from the most searching examination through which I had caused my heart to pass again and again, as to my motives before I began writing, and whilst I was writing; and judging, moreover, from the earnestness of prayer in which I had sought to ascertain the mind of God in the matter, and of the subsequent full assurance which I had of its being according to His will that I should in this way serve the Church—I was almost immediately led to consider this uncomfortable and trying feeling as a temptation, and I therefore went to the box, opened it, brought out some copies, and soon gave one away so that the step could not be retraced. This was the last temptation or struggle I have had of that kind, for I have never since, even for one minute, been allowed to regret publishing the *Narrative*.'

The first legacy received, which arrived at about this time, was rather touching. It was only 6s. 6½d., and was left by a young boy. He had saved up this sum from the various presents of money given him during his illness, and a short while before he died he had asked that the whole of his little treasure might be sent to the

Orphans.

Just before the new Boys' House was due to open, and when he had much unsettled work on his hands, George Müller fell ill again. This time it was his head which troubled him. On November 7th, 1837, he wrote, 'I can work no longer, my head being in such a weak state from continual exertion.' He was much troubled at the thought of being laid aside when there was so much to be done, and new people to be introduced to their duties. 'But', he says, 'the Lord knows better and cares for His work more than I do or can. Therefore I desire to leave the matter with Him.' He and his family went to Weston-super-Mare for a week, returning to Bristol on November 25th, but he was no better. He was ill for several weeks. On Christmas Eve he noted that it was the seventh Sunday that he had been laid aside. In January he and his family went for a change of air to Trowbridge, and while there he read Whitefield's life. He was particularly impressed by Whitefield's custom of reading the Bible on his knees, a practice which he himself had sometimes carried out, but, he now decided, far too little. We have another glimpse of those mighty periods of prayer, noted in his diary while at Trowbridge. 'I have spent several hours in prayer today, and read on my knees, and prayed for two hours over Psalm 63.'

He seems to have been far from well during

most of that Spring, and in April went again to Germany, to assist a friend for the same reasons and in the same way as on his previous visit; also in the hope that a stay in his native air might restore him, and to see his father again. He found the old man much aged, and thought he would not survive another winter. They parted as those who did not expect to meet again on earth, though actually this was not so, and they did meet once more.

'How it would have cheered the separation on both sides, were my dear father a believer! But it made my heart sad indeed to see him, in all human probability for the last time, without having scriptural ground for hope respecting his soul.'

CHAPTER SIX

YEARS OF TESTING

The orphan work continued for about thirteen years after it began in 1836, without any marked change being made, except that in 1844 the fourth house was opened. The first house had been furnished for thirty children and their teachers; the four houses when full, housed 130 people in all.

The first two years brought no great trials of

faith, although by the end of June, 1838, Müller records that nearly a hundred people were in the houses, and needing to be clothed and fed. He and his associates kept to their resolve, as their successors have done ever since, to make no appeals for money, to ask no one individually to give, to put out no advertisements, not even to reveal the state of the funds when asked. At first, the only people who knew the financial position were Müller himself, his wife, his friend and associate Henry Craik, and the master of the Boys' Orphan House, Mr. Thomas, a particularly devout Christian whom Müller early felt led to take into his confidence. These four people gave themselves constantly to secret prayer, both alone and corporately, and money sufficient for the needs of the work came in fairly steadily, though mostly in rather small amounts.

In July, 1838, they began to experience their first real testing. Müller was convinced that God had allowed them to receive immediate answers to prayers for the first two years as an encouragement, but that now the time had arrived when He was to try their faith. These trials continued with little intermission for more than ten years, and were repeated for long periods many times in the Institution's later history.

Chapter Six in the *Autobiography* is headed 'Severe Trials in Early Orphan Work.

1838–1843'. Viewed from the human level a more appropriate title might have been 'Five Years of Hair-Raising Situations'. The Müllers and the Craiks, with no regular salaries nor private means for the support of themselves and their children, depended entirely on the gifts of money, and occasionally of goods, which were sent in answer to their prayers. Most of these were the donations of those who felt called to support them as the Ministers of Bethesda Chapel. Their own incomes, made up in this way, had no connection with any money which might be contributed for the objects of the Scriptural Knowledge Institution. That, alone, was an amazing demonstration of faith. But George Müller made himself responsible, by this same method of believing prayer, for the material needs not only of himself, his wife and child, but for those of a hundred other people also. The living for all of them was frugal, no doubt, but for all except the well-to-do it was a frugal age. Everyone was properly clad, everybody sat down to regular meals in those Orphan Houses. Often and often there would be enough for dinner in all the Houses, but only, perhaps, half the amount of bread required, and no milk, for tea. Then midway through the afternoon someone would call with £1, or perhaps a parcel of second-hand articles would arrive by post and one of the helpers would hasten out to sell them, and bring back money enough to pay for the milk just as the matrons were about to send the milkman away without taking any in. Müller would never incur a debt, however small; all had to be paid for as it was bought. He and his assistants preferred, naturally, that the children should not be given bread on the day it was baked, both for economy's sake and because it was more wholesome for them if not eaten new. Even so, bread might not be taken in unless the money was in hand to pay for it. Many a time was the baker due to arrive, or even at the door, and money came only just in time for it to be purchased.

On one occasion a lady visited the Orphan Houses and spent some time with Müller, asking him many searching questions, as if trying to satisfy herself that all that she had heard about supplies for the orphans were true.

At last she said, 'Tell me, Mr. Müller, does God *really* answer prayer?'

Now, unknown to her, Müller was at that moment completely out of funds. To make the situation even more tense, while they had been talking he had heard the sound of milk churns being handled, and knew that the milkman was below, and that at any moment the matron would come up to ask for money to pay. On the face of things it looked as if he would not only have to instruct the matron to refuse the milk, but be forced to fail in his witness to the faithfulness of God before his sceptical visitor. But with George Müller it was always a case of 'while I breathe I pray', and he was already lifting his heart to God. As the lady was putting her question there came a knock at the door, and the matron came in with the bill in her hand. Now what was Müller to do?

The lady rose to her feet, saying, 'Well, I see you are busy with the affairs of the Institution, and I must not take up any more of your time. But before I go I should like to give you this, if you will kindly accept it,' and she placed ten sovereigns in Müller's hand.

One can imagine his smile of joy at his Father's dependability as he replied: 'You ask me if God always intervenes in time to save us from want. Here is your answer. You have yourself supplied it with your very kind gift.' And as he handed one of the sovereigns to the matron, who took her departure, he told his visitor what had happened.

What is probably the best-known incident in the life of George Müller is mentioned neither in the *Autobiography* nor in the biographies by Pierson or Warne. I have had to rely for details on the only account of it that I have seen in print, which comes in a small paper-covered biographical sketch called *The Adventures of Sister Abigail*. Abigail Luff's father was a close friend of George Müller. The story is told in the following words.

'Early one morning Abigail was playing in Mr. Müller's garden at the Orphanage. Mr. Müller took her hand, saying, "Come, see what our Father will do," and he led her into a long dining-room. The plates and cups or bowls were on the table. There was nothing on the table but empty dishes. There was no food in the larder, and no money to supply the need. The children were standing waiting for their morning meal, when Mr. Müller said, "Children, you know we must be in time for school." Then lifting his hand, said, "Dear Father, we thank Thee for what Thou art going to give us to eat."

A knock at the door was heard. The baker stood there, and said, "Mr. Müller, I couldn't sleep last night. Somehow I felt you didn't have bread for breakfast, and the Lord wanted me to send you some. So I got up at two o'clock and baked some fresh bread, and have brought it."

George Müller thanked the man and praised God for His care, then said, "Children, we not only have bread, but the rare treat of fresh bread." No sooner had he said this than there came a second knock at the door. This time it was the milkman. He announced that his milk cart had broken down right in front of the Orphanage, and that he would like to give the children his cans of fresh milk, so that he could empty his waggon and repair it.'

The greater part of the supply for the

Orphans came direct from gifts, and, as the years went by, from legacies. However, there were many ways in which Müller and his helpers raised small sums of money. Nothing in the Orphan Houses was allowed to be sold if it was needed for the children, but anything that was for the time being superfluous was, in emergency, taken out and sold without delay. On one such occasion Müller recollected some blankets, which had been given but which were not yet required for use, so that they were stored away in one of the houses. He did not believe in hoarding, and the money was urgently needed, so the blankets were brought out and examined. Moths were found in one pair, so he felt confirmed in his notion that he ought to sell rather than store them. Ten pairs were sold, and made £7.

Another minor source of income was the sale of the girls' needlework, which was, of course, merely following the practice of all charitable institutions at that period. Sewing of all descriptions was very carefully taught in the Orphan Houses, and a high standard was maintained, so no doubt the work was readily bought.

Knitting also was one of the regular occupations of both boys and girls, and knitted stockings were sold to augment the funds.

Any little sums of money due to an orphan, such as a debt owing to the parents, paid after that parent's death, were expected to be handed over to the Orphan fund when the child was received into the institution. More than once the answer to that day's pressing needs came in the form of the arrival of a new orphan with perhaps £2 as its 'dowry'. The fact that the said orphan brought not only £2 but another mouth to feed did not disturb George Müller. He had prayed for the supply of his children's needs, and it had been granted. This was sufficient for the day. If God had sent him one more child, then He would undoubtedly send that amount more of food and clothing. And so it always came to pass.

The wonderful devotion, not only of Müller, who during his lifetime gave the greater part of his total income to God's work, but of his assistants also, calls forth the deepest admiration. Repeatedly he records how, in an hour of need, workers in the Orphan Houses would bring him all the money they had, leaving themselves penniless for the time being. Sometimes one of them would offer to work without salary as long as the period of extreme trial should last. No wonder that Müller wrote: 'God be praised for such labourers'. But he was mindful of their needs as much as of those of the children. When £50 arrived one November evening in 1838, he was particularly thankful for it, because it enabled him to pay the overdue salaries. 'Though they are willing to labour

71

without any remuneration, nevertheless "the labourer is worthy of his reward".'

On September 29th, 1838, the rent was due, and there was no money with which to pay it. Twelve o'clock came, and although Müller and one of his friends had prayed from ten until a quarter to twelve, the money did not come. He records that this was the second, and only the second, complete failure as to answers to prayer that they had had in four and a half years. The previous failure had also been of money for rent; in that case of the rent of one of the day-school rooms. He tells how he had had misgivings that they might be disappointed in the rent-money on this occasion, as he had had a feeling that God was leading him to put by money weekly, or even daily, for the purpose. He now felt convinced that he should do so, and resolved accordingly.

The week-end passed, with just enough coming in for supplies for the children, but no more. Then, on Tuesday, money came in from several quarters, and he was able to pay the £19 10s. for the rent, and still have something in hand for present needs.

By 1847 there were a hundred and fifty people to be provided for every day; orphans, teachers and helpers. The humanly-speaking hand-to-mouth existence continued as it had done year after year, but the faith of Müller and his friends never faltered. Again and again he records how he had started a day with nothing at all in the funds, but something always arrived in time for the next meal to be cooked. Sometimes he had some trifling amount, perhaps only a farthing left, which would seem to him like the handful of meal in the barrel. Often on such occasions he would be impelled by some inner urge, which in our day might be called a hunch, to vary his usual procedure without knowing why. He would feel led to walk home by a route different from his customary one, or he would make a detour because he felt chilly and in need of exercise. Then the reason would be made plain to him. He would meet someone who would hand him a couple of sovereigns, or he would arrive on his doorstep just as a stranger came up to proffer ten pounds.

He anticipates the notion that is bound to enter the minds of those who read his *Narrative*, that such a life must be a terrible strain and not at all happy. He says, in 1848, 'I solemnly declare that I do not find this life a trying life, but a very happy life, and I am consequently not in the least tired of it. Straits and difficulties I expected from the beginning ... but cheerfully, for the glory of God and for the profit of God's dear children, did I desire to pass through them, if only the saints might be benefited by the dealings of God with me. The longer I go on in this service, the greater the trials of one kind or another become; but at the same time, the happier am I in this my service, and the more assured that I am engaged as the Lord would have me to be.'

He was not always down to his last penny. On November 9th, 1848, for instance, when all the money was almost spent, £1000 arrived, to be disposed of as most needed, and not infrequently he records receiving £50, £100 or £200 in one donation. But with the other four Objects as well as the Orphanage perpetually needing funds, even such considerable sums cannot have gone very far. The need for the prayer of faith remained a daily one.

One of his most attractive characteristics was the way in which he observed and appreciated the minutest detail. He tells how, on a December day in 1841, a penny saved the situation. At the Boys' Orphan House exactly eightpence was needed to make up the dinner to the required amount, but there was only sevenpence in hand. One of the helpers, having heard that something had on the previous evening been put into the box in the Girls' House, went round to open it. The box contained precisely one penny, and it was recalled that an elderly woman had dropped it in.

By March, 1843, he began to feel that a second house for girls was needed. The vacancies in the first house were so quickly taken up that it was becoming impossible to move up the older children from the Infants' House to the Girls' House at the appropriate age, as there was not room for them. He knew two sisters who seemed to be just the people to take charge of the new house, and also he had at the time £300 in hand which could be used for furnishing and fitting it up.

He said nothing to anyone, but gave himself to prayer for guidance in the matter. He prayed for twenty-two days before he mentioned it even to his wife. On the 24th day, assured now that it was God's will that he should go forward, he entered into negotiations for renting Number 4, Wilson Street. In June the house was fitted up, and in July the first children were received into it.

A thought that naturally rises in the mind is, whether it was not very undermining to the orphans' sense of security not to know where the money for the next meal was coming from. The answer is, simply, that they knew nothing about the situation. Only Müller and his intimates knew the state of the funds, which circle was enlarged after a year or two to include all the teachers and helpers so that they might be privileged to share in the prayers of faith. The children were not told anything. Their meals, though plain, were regular, and never failed to appear. Müller says in November 1839, 'During the whole of this week, greatly as we have been tried, and though twice no stock of bread could be taken in, yet there has been nourishing food at every meal, and neither the children nor any other person can have perceived our poverty'.

He uses one of those occasions when he started the day with a farthing, and adequate means arrived in time to pay that day's expenses, as an illustration of God's care for all who trust in Him. He addresses himself to all, to whatever class of society they may belong, who find it hard to pay their way. He pictures the working man, with many children and small wages, or one of the middle class with extremely limited means.

He reminds them that God loves all of us. May not they, he asks, under their trials, do as he and his friends do? He assures them that God is willing to help all His children who put their trust in Him. They must not think that because they are not called upon to establish orphanages, that they are not warranted to rely upon God in all their need. 'Nor are you to suppose,' he says, 'that our only trials in this work arise from want of means, so that in carrying it on, we have to rely upon God for nothing besides this. I assure you that the want of means is the smallest trial, and that I have had far, far greater exercises of faith on account of other things in connection with this work than those arising from the want of means. But the trials connected with the want of means I dwell on so particularly, because that is a matter which can be understood by all, and in which the senses themselves almost force us, so to speak, to acknowledge the hand of God'.

An incident which illustrates differing viewpoints in the matter of raising money for religious purposes is recorded under the date May 21st, 1844. Two people were going from door to door in the street where Müller lived, collecting money to pay off a chapel debt. He describes how he remonstrated with them, considering that such a procedure dishonoured God's name. 'I sought to show them,' he says, 'that if their work were of God He would, in answer to their prayers, send them help: and if not, ought they not to give up what was not His work, and not force the matter by calling promiscuously from house to house upon believers and unbelievers?' They replied that as the gold and silver are the Lord's they called upon the unconverted for help for His work. He answered that just because the silver and gold were the Lord's, there was no need to go to His enemies for the support of His work. He failed to convince them, and they went on their way. He turned his attention to the post, which had just come in. It brought eleven pounds, and added to £1 1s. 5d. which had been taken out of the boxes in the Orphan Houses, made up the sum of £12 1s. 5d., all of which had arrived at his house while he was talking to the two collectors.

On December 22nd he writes: '*A solemn day*. I received today the information from my father that my brother died on October 7th. When I saw him in April this year, he was living in open sin and disunion with my father. I cannot learn that his end was different from his life, so that I have no comfort in his death. Of all the trials that can befall a believer, the death of an unconverted near relative seems to me one of the greatest. "Shall not the judge of all the earth do right?" must be the stay of the believer at such a time and, by grace, it is my stay now.'

In February, 1840, he visited Germany, and saw his father once more. There seems to have been much mutual affection shown. 'How cheerfully should I have left him this morning, did I know him to be safe in Jesus. But alas! he as yet is not resting upon Christ, though he is so far religious as to read prayers and the Bible.'

On April 7th he received the news from his little half-brother that his father had died on March 30th. Again his great sorrow was that there was no evidence that the old man died in the faith of Christ. 'Every true believer who has unconverted parents, for whose spiritual welfare he is concerned, can understand what joy it would have been to me to have heard a satisfactory account of a true change of heart in my dear father before his end... During no period did I pray more frequently or more earnestly for the conversion of my dear aged parent, than during the last year of his life, but, at all events, it did not please the Lord to let me *see* the answer to my prayers.'

CHAPTER SEVEN

ASHLEY DOWN

From the time of the first opening of the Orphan Houses, George Müller had been looking about for more suitable premises to rent in Bristol or its immediate neighbourhood, as the Wilson Street houses had many disadvantages. He had never thought of building, however, as he had always felt that any money sent for the orphans should be spent on present necessities. A sentence in the *Narrative* aptly expresses his outlook at that period (1845). 'The pilgrim character of the Christian seems lost in building.' But when he was just forty, he received, on October 30th, 1845, a letter from a Wilson Street resident, which brought the matter before him in a new aspect. It was, he tells us, a friendly communication, the writer merely stating in a courteous manner that he and the other neighbours were in many ways inconvenienced

79

by the presence in the street of the four Orphan Houses.

Müller happened to be very much occupied during the week when the letter came, but on the following Monday morning he set apart some hours to think over and to pray about the problem. In his precise, clear-thinking German fashion, he wrote down the pros and cons, and set himself to weigh them carefully against each other. The main reasons which occurred to him for removing from Wilson Street were as follows:

1. The noise made by the children in their play hours was a nuisance to the neighbours. Müller felt this to be a just complaint, as, on reflection, he realized that he himself would find the noise trying to his head if he lived next door to the playground.
2. The drains were inadequate for use by such numbers.
3. There was only one playground between the four houses, so that the children had to use it by turns.
4. There was no land for cultivation, which was a serious lack, as the boys did not have any opportunity to learn gardening, or to work out of doors.
5. There was not enough space in the Wilson Street houses for all of the washing to be

done at home, and most had to be sent out. This was an expense, and the older girls were deprived of what would have been useful training for their lives in service later.

6. The air in Wilson Street was not bracing enough for children such as the orphans, most of whom came of delicate or even diseased parents.

7. The staff had no garden or other open space near at hand, where they might go for a breath of fresh air when off duty.

8. In times of sickness, the Wilson Street houses were too cramped.

9. Even at ordinary times, it would be desirable to have more room.

The reasons against moving from Wilson Street it is not necessary to list, as they were very slight.

Müller recognized that if he moved, he would have to build. That same afternoon he laid the matter before eight of his fellow-workers in the Church. They all thought he should leave Wilson Street, and saw no reasons against building. For the next three days he and his wife met together for prayer about the matter, and he became sure that it was God's will. He and his friends began asking the Lord for the means to build, which he perceived must amount to at least £10,000, as he intended to put up a building to hold 300 orphans.

They went on praying for fifteen days, and not a single donation towards the building fund came in, but Müller was not discouraged. He was now so perfectly certain that it was God's will that he should build, that he was, he says, as full assured that the Lord would give the means as if he had already seen the new premises actually before him.

Thirty-five days passed by from that on which he had begun to pray for the money, and on the thirty-sixth he received £1,000 towards the building fund. This was the largest single donation he had ever received up to that time, but he relates that he was as calm as though he had only received a shilling, because his heart was looking out for answers. On December 29th, came the second donation, this time for £50. After that, for three years, the money began to flow in, sometimes in large amounts, often in small ones, until by June, 1848, the money in hand exceeded ten thousand pounds, more than enough to begin operations. Müller had resolved that the work should not be started until all the money required had been received. He had estimated that the purchase of the land itself, enough for the house and for cultivation, would cost between £2,000 and £3,000. Land round Bristol at that time was becoming expensive, as speculators were buying it up with so much building going on in all directions. The house itself he expected to cost from £6,000 to £8,000 and the furnishing and fittings about £1,500.

It was on February 3rd, 1846, that he heard of suitable and cheap land on Ashley Down, which turned out, when he went to inspect it, to be the most promising of any that he had seen. On February 4th he called on the owner, but failed to discover him either at home or at his office. He might have called again later, but decided that God's hand was in his not finding him at either place, and so decided not to force the matter. Next day he had an interview with the man, who told him that he had lain awake during the night, his mind occupied about the piece of land, having been informed that George Müller had been inquiring about it. He had decided that if Mr. Müller should apply for it, he would let him have it for £120 per acre, instead of the £200 which he had previously asked. The agreement was made that morning, and Müller purchased a field of seven acres on Ashley Down, which name was to become world-famous by association with his own.

A London architect, Foster by name, whose firm later was known as Foster, Wood and Awdry, had offered to make the plan for the new Orphan House, and also to superintend the building, free of charge. On February 19th he came down from London to look at the site. He reported it to be very suitable as to situation, drainage and water.

On July 6th, Müller was given the largest donation he had so far received, the sum of £2,050. 'It is impossible to describe my joy in God when I received this donation. I was neither excited nor surprised; for I look out for answers to my prayers. I believe that God hears me. Yet my heart was so full of joy that I could only sit before God, and admire Him, like David in 2 Samuel vii. At last I cast myself flat on my face, and burst forth in thanksgiving to God, and in surrendering my heart afresh to Him for His blessed service.'

On July 5th, 1847, building was begun. During February, 1849, £2,000 was given in a single donation towards the furnishings. As the new house was to accommodate three hundred children, instead of the hundred and twenty at present under his care, Müller placed orders for thousands of yards of material for all the new clothes that would be needed. A donation of £300 enabled him to order stocks of provisions and other things on wholesale terms. By March 31st, he was able to write: 'After all the expenses had been met for the purchase of the land, the conveyance of the same, the enrolment of the trust deeds in Chancery, the building, fitting-up and furnishing of the New Orphan House, there remained a balance of £776 14s. 3½d., affording a manifest proof that the Lord can not only supply us with all we need in His service, simply in answer to prayer, but that He can even give us even more than we need.'

The New Orphan House was opened, and the three hundred places were soon filled with the children who had been moved there from the old houses in Wilson Street and an even larger number of newcomers. George Müller now had an enormous amount of work on his hands, as everything was under his close personal surveillance. In the account books and other records of those days his writing is constantly in evidence. His correspondence of about 3,000 letters a year he accomplished without a secretary. Besides the work of the Orphan House, the other four Objects of the Scriptural Knowledge Institution claimed his attention. He had also his pastoral work at Bethesda Chapel to take up much time and energy. He admits that with the opening of the new house on Ashley Down he became so busy that he was separated from home and wife and daughter more than ever, as he was for most of the day at the orphanage, and even spent the night there sometimes. Nevertheless, even so soon as the end of the year 1850 he began to feel conscious of the call to build a second Orphanage, larger than the first. He felt that he should house another 700 children, making a thousand altogether. As before, he kept the thought in his heart, for many months, telling no one what he was contemplating, but praying daily for guidance. Among the reasons that impelled him forward was the knowledge that there were multitudes of destitute orphan children. In 1845 an official report had stated that in the prisons of England alone there were six thousand orphans under eight years old. He longed to be instrumental in preventing parentless children from suffering such a fate. The only reason against extending the work that really weighed with him was the thought that he might be going beyond his physical and mental strength. He writes, 'I might say, that it is the only real difficulty. This, too, however, I am enabled to put aside and overcome thus: by husbanding my strength, by great order, by regular habits, by lightening the work as much as possible, and by using every help I can, I have been enabled to get through a vast quantity of work... The entire management and direction, and the whole vast correspondence of the Institution, has devolved upon myself alone these sixteen years and ten months, and I have been thinking that, by seeking an efficient secretary, an efficient clerk and an inspector of the schools, I might, with God's help, accomplish yet more, though much of what I have been doing hitherto would need to be done by others.'

These did not remain mere thoughts; they passed into actions. More and more he learnt to delegate his work to others, and so was able to build and direct the activities of not one more Orphan House, but four more. The sums of money involved were colossal. In envisaging this second House, he realized that the land and building would cost at least £35,000, and that, when it was occupied, more than £7,000 annually would be needed to keep it going. Nor was there any money in hand to start the new fund, as the first Orphan House was absorbing all that was at the moment available. He admits that regarding the matter on the natural level, he might well tremble. But George Müller recognized two viewpoints: the natural and the spiritual. To the ordinary person this is likely to be tinged with unreality, to suggest a mere pious phrase. That the spiritual approach was the objective one was borne out by events. He had surely been right when he stated that on the natural plane there was no possibility of raising the enormous sums of money required. No appeals, no money-raising schemes, could have brought in a tenth of what was eventually expended for the Orphans. With a faith as absolute as has surely ever been exhibited, Müller kept his mind and soul fixed on the promises of God, unwavering in his certainty that God would honour them. His faith was vindicated, by the bricks and mortar of the five great Orphan Houses that he raised on Ashley Down, and even more in the lives of the ten thousand children whom he rescued from destitution and brought up as Christians during his own lifetime, not to mention the number, nearly as large, that has passed through the Homes since his death.

When he was weighing up the reasons for and against building a second house on Ashley Down, he imagined himself being challenged with the question, 'Suppose now, you were even to succeed in getting this large Orphan House built, how will you provide for 700 other orphans?' He answers: 'There is much weight in the objection, looking at it *naturally*. I am too much a man of business, and too much a person of calm, quiet, cool calculation, not to feel its force. And indeed, were I only to look at the thing *naturally*, I should at once be ready to own that I am going too far; for the increase of expenditure for the support of these 700 other orphans could not be less than eight thousand pounds a year more, so that the current expenses of the Institution, reckoning its present state, and including those eight thousand pounds, would be about fifteen thousand pounds a year. Now I am free to own that I have no human prospect of obtaining such a sum year by year. But while matters stand thus, looking at them naturally, I see no difficulty at all in them spiritually. If according to the will of God I am enabled to go about this intended second Orphan House; and if, with His help, I shall be enabled to finish it, He will surely provide for those who are gathered together in it, as long as He shall enable me to trust in Him for supplies.'

He was weeks in prayer for guidance about this second House before he even told his wife, and then weeks longer before he laid the matter before an old and valued friend. He gave him the manuscript in which he had set down all his reasons for and against building. This friend read it, and when he returned it gave a favourable verdict, and half a sovereign to start the new fund.

This was a great encouragement to Müller, coming from what he described as a 'cautious, judicious and prayerful man of God.' He proceeded to make his intention publicly known, and the next day received a sovereign from a lady. A certain amount was contributed, including £500 in one day, but in four months only a fortieth part (£882 18s. 6d.) had come in. On September 13th not one penny came for the Building Fund, but five more orphans arrived, all very destitute. He was nothing daunted, but continued to pray and to look out for the means which he was quite certain would come. It was the host of children awaiting admission which encouraged him to continue to wait upon God. On March 17th, 1852, he records that the previous year 170 children had been awaiting admission, and since then 183 more had been applied for, and of these 353 he had only had vacancies for 27.

Large sums came from time to time, which naturally encouraged him. In January, 1853, there came in one day £8,100, the joint donation of several Christians. In January, 1854, another large donation amounted to £5,207, and in January, 1855, another gift of £5,700 was promised him, and paid in instalments by the middle of April. So the money came in, sometimes in large sums, more often in small ones, all through the years, until the five houses stood on Ashley Down, where there they have remained for all the world to see ever since, a silent witness to the truth that God hears and answers prayer.

These are the details concerning the building of the five Houses:

Number 1, on its site of seven acres, cost about £15,000, which included the purchase of the land, legal expenses, building, fitting up and furnishing. It was opened in June, 1849, and housed 300 children, with the staff to teach and care for them.

Number 2 was opened, on land next to that on which Number 1 was built, on November 12th, 1857. It housed 400 children and cost over £21,000.

Number 3 was built on a site of $11\frac{1}{2}$ acres, on the opposite side of the road from the other two houses. It was opened on March 12th, 1862, housed 450 children, and cost over £23,000.

Numbers 4 and 5 were planned for by Mr. Müller at the same time. They were built on a site of 18½ acres, adjoining that on which Number 2 stands, but round the corner from it. Between them they housed 900 children. Number 4 was opened on November 5th, 1868, and Number 5 on January 6th, 1870. Together they cost over £50,000.

CHAPTER EIGHT

FINANCIAL

The state of the finances of all of George Müller's projects varied considerably over the years. It will be remembered how for the first two years of the orphan work, supplies, if not copious, were at least fairly regular. Then followed the years of great trial, during which Müller and his associates had their faith tested to the utmost, and the whole Institution (comprising the first four Objects and the Orphan Houses), was running almost on a day-to-day basis. However, from 1848 money began to come in far more plentifully, and from that date until 1874 funds were reasonably abundant, in spite of the enormous extension of the Orphan work during those years, from 130 orphans in Müller's care in 1848, to 2,050 in

1874.

From 1874 to 1885 large sums came in for the orphans, including one legacy of over £11,000, but with the equivalent of the population of a small town to be fed, clothed, housed and started in life, even very big legacies or donations were soon spent. At times during these years funds became very short, and often days would go by without enough coming in to keep the Institution running for even one day. In 1874 Müller wrote: 'But God, our infinitely rich Treasurer, remains to us. It is this which gives me peace. Moreover if it pleases Him, with a work requiring about £44,000 a year, to make me do again at the evening of my life, what I did for Him from August 1838 to April, 1849, I am not only prepared for it, but again would I gladly pass through all these trials of faith with regard to means, if He only might be glorified, and His Church and the world benefited. Often and often this last point has of late passed through my mind, and I have placed myself in the position of having no means at all left; and 2,100 persons, not only daily at the table, but with everything else, to be provided for, and all the funds gone; 189 missionaries to be assisted, and nothing whatever left; about one hundred schools with 9,000 scholars in them, to be entirely supported, and no means for them in hand; about four million Tracts and tens of thousands of copies of the Holy

Scriptures yearly now to be sent out, and all the money expended. Invariably, however, with this probability before me, I have said to myself: God, who has raised up this work through me, God who has led me generally year after year to enlarge it; God who has supported this work now for more than forty years, will still help, and will not suffer me to be confounded, because I rely upon Him. I commit the whole work to Him, and He will provide me with what I need, in future also, though I know not whence the means are to come.' Having quoted the above paragraph in the *Report*, he then adds, 'This I wrote in my Journal on July 28th. The reader will now feel interested in learning how we fared under these circumstances. I therefore make further extracts from my Journal.' Then follow details of the income for the next two or three months. That of September totalled £11,309 4s. 5½d. This included a single gift of £5,327 7s. 6d. from a man who Müller never saw, though he had long been a generous contributor.

The story of another donation is worth recording in detail, as it shows the extent of the self-sacrifice which poor people would make for God's work, and also reveals the extreme care which Müller would take to go deeply into a case of this kind to satisfy himself that he did right in accepting the money. On August 9th, 1853, he received £88 2s. 6d. from a certain

Christian man, the proceeds of an 'Orphan-Box' in the small place of worship of which he was a member. These 'Orphan-Boxes', which are referred to from time to time in the *Narrative*, were not issued by George Müller and his associates, nor sent out from the Orphan Houses. They were purely private affairs, placed in chapels and meeting-houses, or in private houses, to collect money for the Orphans. The setting up of such a box was in each case the idea of those who did it, and the box was provided locally.

In this case the box was opened to reveal over £93 2s. 6d.; the three pounds odd being the combined contributions of various people, and the £90 that of a poor widow, who had recently sold her house, her only property, for that sum. She had put the money into the box unperceived, but she was known to have sold her house, and to have mentioned to someone that she meant to send the money to Mr. Müller. The chapel treasurer felt he could not take the money without remonstrance, and sent two friends to talk to her. She was known to be very poor, and they feared that she might afterwards regret her action. They managed to prevail upon her to take back five pounds, but no more, and the treasurer could not do otherwise than forward the rest of the money to Bristol. On reading the treasurer's letter, George Müller felt as he did about it, and therefore wrote to the widow, inviting her to come and see him, and offering to pay her travelling expenses. The widow, a woman of sixty, arrived, and told him just how she had come to do as she had done; how she had resolved, if ever she came into possession of the house, to sell it, and give the proceeds to the Lord. Müller questioned her carefully, trying to discover whether she had acted on a wave of enthusiasm, but she told him that she had made the decision ten years previously. Confident now that she had not given the money on impulse, he then pointed out that as she was poor and no longer young, might she not keep the money for herself? Her reply was, 'God has always provided for me and I have no doubt he will do so in the future also. I am able to work and earn my bread as well as others, and am willing to work as a nurse or in any other way.' What, says Müller, could he say against this? It was just what a child of God would say, and should say. He then inquired what she wished him to do with the money. She said that she would like best for it to be used for the support of missionaries. She also wished Mr. Müller himself to have part of the money. This he absolutely refused to do. 'I then prayed with this dear, godly woman, commended her to God, separated from her, and have not seen her since.' But he had not quite finished with the matter even now. He kept the money by him, and seven months later he wrote to her once more, offering her back the whole of the £85 or a part of it, but her reply convinced him finally that she really meant what she said, so he took the money to aid the foreign missionaries, as she had requested.

One other instance of the generosity of poor and lonely women may be given. During 1855, Müller and his fellow workers went through another lean time. Then on October 17th, a stranger called to see Mr. Müller, to hand over to him £1 for the orphans and £200 for foreign missions. These sums were both from an elderly woman, whose whole life savings made up the £200. She had recently had left to her an annual income of £30, and felt constrained, for love of Christ, to give her entire savings for the foreign missions. She had never had more than £6 a year wages in all her life, out of which she had for many years sent £1 or more for the Orphans.

Müller records several instances of gifts which had been made possible because the senders had given up some luxury. A commercial traveller came across one of the *Reports* in a hotel where he was spending the night, read it, and there and then decided to break with the commercial-room custom of taking wine at dinner. In nine months he saved £4 7s. 0d., which he forwarded to Ashley Down. A workman, also after reading a *Report*, denied himself beer and sent £5 for the

Orphans' Christmas pudding. Another man sent £20, 'saved by not smoking cigars last year.'

From time to time George Müller found it necessary to make a statement refuting various false ideas connected with the funds of the Scriptural Knowledge Institution. He would set down some of the notions that he found to be prevalent, and comment on each. One reason often alleged to account for his success in raising money was that he was a foreigner, to which he makes the obvious retort that this might be expected to be a hindrance rather than a help. Another suggestion put forward was 'the novelty of the thing', which rather lost force when more than twenty years had passed since the work was started, as he pointed out when writing in 1858. At that date, too, the total sum given since the beginning of the enterprise was more than £113,000. This made another idea, that he had access to some secret treasure, singularly unlikely. He admitted, however, that there was a certain truth in this notion, as he had, through prayer, access to the inexhaustible treasury of God, though it was not that to which his detractors referred.

The fourth and last objection that he mentioned on that occasion, which had more reason in it than the previous ones, was that his success was all due to the *Reports*. To this he replied: 'There is nothing unusual in writing reports. This is done by public institutions generally, but the constant complaint is that the reports are not read. Our *Reports* are not extraordinary as to the power of language, or striking appeals to feelings. They are simple statements of facts. These *Reports* are not accompanied by personal applications for means; but they are simply sent to the donors, or to any other individuals who wish to have or to purchase them. If they produce results, which reports generally do not, I can only ascribe it to the Lord.' The *Reports* always referred to a state of affairs that was past, so that no one could tell the present state of the funds by reading them.

On December 31st each year it was Müller's custom to record the sum total of the money that had been given or sent to him for his own personal use. In 1854 this was £697 11s. 5d., and he writes that he can imagine readers of the Report exclaiming at the amount, in view of the fact that not one clergyman in twenty, and not one minister in a hundred, had an annual income in any way comparable. He is ready to agree that his way of obtaining his material necessities is indeed a happy one. But he says, he has not lived by faith for so long without perceiving one essential truth, and this he underlines in case any of his readers might be thinking that here was an easy way to get a large income. Those who want to go this way must not merely *say* that they trust in God; they must really *do* so. Those who say that they are living by faith, and then take every opportunity to let others know their needs, are not trusting in God. They must tell their needs to God only. They must be willing to have plenty of money, or scarcely anything, as God wills. They must not be too proud to accept a small sum, such as a single shilling, gracefully. They must not hoard what God sends, but share what He gives them with others in need.

In the year 1886 Müller felt moved to record both his income, and the amounts he had felt led to give away of that income, year by year from 1831 to 1885. Having so often written about stewardship, systematic giving, and not laying up treasures on earth, and about the material and spiritual blessings that were sure to follow from acting on such principles, he now felt that a detailed account of his own finances would prove the truth of what he had never failed to assert.

It is important, here as elsewhere, when studying Müller's own account of his actions, not to forget that the over-ruling desire of his life was to demonstrate that God really does answer prayer. Thus he gives facts and figures which, published with any other motive, might seem to be disobeying the divine command to give alms in secret. But no one, considering Müller's life as a whole, could suspect that he was seeking the applause of men.

His personal income, which was derived entirely from unsolicited gifts, for he never received any kind of salary after 1831, rose steadily, with the exception of only a very few years, from £151 in 1831 to more than £2,000 in 1870, after which it varied between £1,417 in 1882 to £4,260 in 1877. Of these vast sums, he retained about £300 a year for himself and his family, the rest being given, by the glad consent of all of them, to various causes: the funds of the Scriptural Knowledge Institution, including the Orphan Houses, missionary work, and so on; to fellow-Christians in need; also to non-Christians; and occasionally to relatives in similar plight.

What about making provision for his family in the event of his death? He attended to that, but not by the ordinary methods. Here is what he wrote on the subject, referring to Mary, his wife:

'I well remember how many times I said to her and our beloved daughter, "My dears, if the Lord should take me away before you, and you should ever be in need of anything, ask the Lord, in childlike simplicity, that He would graciously be pleased to repay you a little of that which I gave to the poor, or to His work, and you will find how, without fail, He will do so".'

In 1856, he received a hundred pounds, the donor's request being that he should use it to start a fund for his support in old age. 'This kind and well-intentioned proposal by the donor (who has since died) appeared to me to be a subtle temptation laid for me (though far from being intended so by him) to depart from the principle on which I had been acting for twenty-six years.' This is how he replied:

My dear Sir,
I hasten to thank you for your kind communication, and to inform you that your cheque for £100 has safely come to hand.

I have no property whatever, nor has my dear wife; nor have I had one shilling regular salary as minister of the Gospel for the last 26 years, nor as Director of the Orphan House and the other Objects of the Scriptural Knowledge Institution. When I am in need of anything I fall on my knees, and ask God that He would be pleased to give me what I need; and He puts it into the heart of someone or other to help me. Thus all my wants have been amply supplied during the last 26 years, and I can say, to the praise of God, I have lacked nothing. My dear wife and my only child, a daughter 24 years old, are of the same mind. Of this blessed way of living none of us is tired, but we become day by day more convinced of its blessedness.

I have never thought it right to make provision for myself, or my dear wife and daughter, except in this way, that when I have seen a case of need, such as an aged widow, a sick person, or helpless infant, I have used the means freely which God has given me, fully believing that if either myself, or my dear wife or daughter at some time or other should be in need of anything, God would richly repay what was given to the poor considering it as lent to Himself.

He then explained that he could not take the hundred pounds to provide for his own or his family's future. He could accept gifts either to himself personally or for his work only for present use, not as endowments. Then after assuring the donor of his appreciation, he suggested holding the cheque until he heard from him again. His correspondent at once wrote back to ask him to use the money for the orphans; next day he sent a second £100, and four days afterwards a third.

His family fully shared his views on the matter. After his wife Mary's death he wrote: 'I so well remember that I used to tell my beloved departed wife that I had put £100 or £200, or less, or more, as the case might be, to the Building Fund of the Orphan Houses, or to Missions, how she would, with an affectionate smile, say, 'Thank you, my dear.' In another place he records that his daughter, in the same circumstances, always showed great delight, as her mother had done.

His second wife, Susannah, was also at one with him on the subject. Writing of the year 1872, he says, 'I had now a companion in my beloved second wife, who shared my joy when I sent anything to the poor, or gave it away otherwise. She had lost the property she once possessed, which among other reasons fitted her the better to be my wife; for if she had been rich, she would not have suited me. I own it freely, that I had joy in the thought that she possessed no property, and that I could make her to share with me in the abundance with which it pleased the Lord to bless me year after year. But after I had made her an offer, I found that she had £200 left, which she gave me, before our marriage, for the Lord's work; thus it is seen that in this respect she was of one mind with me.' The second Mrs. Müller received several considerable legacies after her marriage, three of which account for the income of over £4000 recorded for 1883, and another legacy of over £2000 came to her in 1884. But the Müllers merely increased their donations to the various causes, and continued to live on a small income.

He has some general remarks to make about his own attitude to money. 'If I were left to myself, I should even now, after all the experience I have had, become a lover of money, and hold it fast, and seek to increase my possessions more and more; for I am naturally a calculating business man.' But grace was in possession of his heart, and he viewed all life from the standpoint of heaven. When he thought of Bethlehem and Calvary, gratitude constrained him to give back gladly of that which had so freely been given to him.

He did not believe in maintaining an over-scrupulous attitude towards money. 'The reader would be mistaken if he supposed that, as soon as the Lord has sent me means, my aim is to seek to get rid of them as fast as possible, as if it were a crime to possess a ten-pound note. That is not at all my way of acting. All I seek after, is to have grace, not to hold anything as my own, but as belonging to the Lord; so that whether I have much or little, I desire to look on the much or little as a steward would, not as an owner.'

He imagines his Christian readers saying that it is a blessed way to live, and delightful to be able to give away so much. He agrees, and asks them to try it for themselves, but warns them to keep at it steadily, under all circumstances, and not to waste the Lord's means by keeping up too high a standard of living. 'I have not only allowed myself and family all the necessities, but the conveniences of life; I do this still, if not even more, as I am increasing in years; but I have ever guarded against extravagance in any way, lest my stewardship should be taken from me.'

How did this method of providing for himself and his family turn out in the end? They lived in reasonable comfort all their lives. He outlived both of his wives and his daughter, and ended his days in Orphan House Number 3. His personal estate, including the value of books and household furniture, was sworn at £160 9s. 4d. In all his life, since 1831, he had given away £81,490 18s. 8d.

It occurred to me that although Müller and his successors never advertised the needs of the Institution, nevertheless this might have been done against their will and without their knowledge by well-wishers, and possibly even more by ill-wishers who were out to discredit them. I was therefore not at all surprised to come upon the following, in the 1908 *Report*, addressed to the Director at that time.

Dear Mr. Bergin,

I feel constrained to write to you in connection with an appeal made in a London Sunday newspaper. I feel certain that you know nothing concerning the person who makes the appeal. It was brought to my notice by an unbeliever in a factory where I am engaged, and, of course, this quickly spread among those who despise eternal things, especially as you profess to appeal to none but the living God. I sought to show them that the appeal was made against your principles, and without your knowledge or consent. I shall be greatly delighted to receive a line from you refuting entirely this appeal as having emanated from you. I enclose the appeal:

Müller's 2,000 Orphans. An APPEAL to Friends at Home and Abroad for Donations (none too small) by a Friend. Please send direct to Mr. Fred Bergin, Ashley Down, Bristol, England.

Mr. Bergin hastened to return an answer, to assure the writer that the advertisement had of course been inserted without his knowledge or consent, and to state that should any gifts come as a result, they would be returned to the donors as having been given under a false impression, so that they could not be accepted. One shares his suspicions that the 'friend' is more probably an enemy, and sympathizes with his obvious disquiet. This particular advertisement had been brought to his notice, so that he could take steps to undo some of the harm it might have done, but how was he to know whether many similar ones might not have appeared from time to time in different parts of the world, of which he would never hear, but which might nevertheless seem to give the lie to the principles on which the Institution was founded?

George Müller's Missionary Tours covered the years from 1875 to 1892, and at one period some of his Christian friends wanted him to give them up because at that time the income had fallen off, and they put this fact down to his being absent so much from Bristol. But he could not agree with them, because whenever he returned to Bristol he found everything continuing under his son-in-law's direction as efficiently as it had when he himself had been the sole director. Also, as he points out, in the third year of his tours the income was the largest that it had ever been in all the forty-four years that the work had been in existence. He could pray as effectually for means when he was abroad as when he was at home, and he was always kept posted as to the state of affairs in Bristol by his son-in-law, who wrote to him every week. It was not until he had been on tour every year for nine years that real trials over funds began to be experienced again. The last thirteen years of his life were as challenging to his faith as had been those years from 1838 to 1848, and of these thirteen years the last six, when he had given up his overseas preaching work for good, were the hardest of all.

It seemed as if God were purposely withholding answers to prayer for a time, and instead of there being a falling off of money as soon as George Müller was removed from the earthly scene, matters fell out otherwise. Soon after his death the income increased again, and this is just what he himself would have wished. It seemed to show that it was not his personality which had attracted contributions, nor was it necessary that he should be the one to pray for supplies. The prayers of other believers might be, and evidently were, just as effective. It bore out his reiterated statement that the Orphan Houses were not his Orphan Houses (and he would never allow them to be called after his name) but God's. The work was God's, and He would care for it, so long as His people were faithful in prayer according to the promises of the Bible.

Only a year before his death, on February 12th, 1897, he wrote, 'The first two deliveries did not bring in one single penny in all the many letters I had. During this week we have had to expend more than £1,000 and our income is exceedingly small, and has been so for some time. I do not remember one single day, for more than forty years, when the first two deliveries of letters brought nothing at all. We have now arranged to have, from this day, six united prayer meetings for the helpers, instead of three a week, as for years past; for we expect that more united prayer, more exercise of faith, and more patience, will bring more help. There have been many legacies left, and some are long overdue, but they remain unpaid.'

The financial strain continued almost, though not quite, to the day of his death. In the *Autobiography* his last reference to the money situation is given under March 1st, 1898. 'For about twenty-one months with scarcely the least intermission, the trial of our faith and patience has continued. Today the Lord has refreshed our hearts. This afternoon came in, for the Lord's work, £1,427 1s. 7d., as part payment of a legacy of the late Mrs. E. C. S. For three years and ten months this money has been in the Irish Chancery Court. Hundreds of petitions have been brought before the Lord regarding it, and now, at last, this portion of the total legacy has been received.'

These are the statistics of the income of the Scriptural Knowledge Institution from its beginning in 1834 until George Müller's death in March, 1898:

For the Orphans—£988,829 0s. 10½d.
For the School, Bible, Missionary and
Tract Funds, by voluntary
contributions—£392,341 18s. 7d.

The total of the above is £1,381,170 19s. 5½d. all given in answer to prayer without personal application ever having been made to anyone, and without advertising. Besides the above were the following additions to the income:

By the sale of Bibles, £22,123 1s. 3½d.

By the sale of Tracts, £25,474 4s. 4d.

By the payment of the children in the Day Schools, £24,745 8s. 2d.

The number of Orphans cared for in the Homes from April, 1836 until May, 1898, was ten thousand and twenty-four.

CHAPTER NINE

FAMILY AFFAIRS

Müller and his wife placed their twelve-year-old daughter at a boarding-school in 1844, intending, of course, to pay her fees in the ordinary way. When Lydia had been six months at the school, her father asked the headmistress for the account. The lady, who was a sincere Christian, and no doubt well aware of Müller's way of life and work for the orphans, replied that it was a pleasure to her to educate his daughter without fee. Müller pressed the matter, however, obtained the account and paid it. The exact sum was returned to him anonymously, and he soon found out that it was from Lydia's headmistress. From that time onwards, he said, he could never again obtain the account, although Lydia remained at the school for six years. He accepted the situation, feeling thus about it: 'God had laid it on my heart to care about poor destitute orphans. To this service I had been led to give myself; He, in return, as a recompense even for this life, took care that my own beloved child should have a very good education, free of expense to me. I was able, and well able, to pay for her education, and most willing to do so; but the Lord gave it gratuitously; thus showing how ready He is abundantly to help me and to supply my wants.'

On April 29th, 1846, when Lydia was thirteen and a half, her parents had 'the inexpressibly great joy' of receiving the following letter from her. Only part of the letter is quoted:

My very dear Father and Mother,
I am so very glad that you are better... Dearest Father and Mother, I wished to tell you that I was now happy, but I have not liked to, and thought I could better tell you in writing than by speaking. I do not know exactly the time when I first was happy in the prospect of death and eternity, but I know that the work of God in my heart was very gradual. I can now say, 'Thanks be unto God for His unspeakable gift'. Please dear Father and Mother to pray for me, that I may be kept from dishonouring God, and that I may

be more and more thankful to Him for the gift of His Son, and for my dear parents, my dear Aunty, and my dear teachers, and all kind friends who love and pray for me. And now dear Father and Mother with much love, I remain your affectionate little daughter, Lydia Müller.

Her father made her wait a few months longer, and then at the end of 1846 she was baptized and received into Communion at the age of fourteen years and three months.

In the year 1853 Lydia, then aged twenty, contracted typhus fever, and by the beginning of July, after a fortnight's illness, seemed beyond recovery. Her father and mother met this trial, described by Müller as the severest through which they had ever passed, with their customary faith. When I read his account of the experience, I was impressed by its close similarity to one that occurred among my personal acquaintances. The sufferer in this other case was a girl of thirteen. Her parents, an Anglican clergyman and his wife, held a religious outlook somewhat different from that of the Müllers, but they were, like them, people of dedicated life. The parents in both cases adopted the same course: they completely surrendered their child to God, for life or for death, as seemed best to Him. For both, the outcome was the same. The daughter started to recover from that moment, and in due course regained her normal health.

On January 22nd, 1866, Henry Craik, who had been George Müller's friend and fellow-worker for thirty-six years, died after an illness of seven months, when both men were just over sixty years of age. Müller himself was ill at the time, and remained in poor health for three months afterwards, no doubt greatly missing his old friend with whom he had always been able to talk over every problem.

Four years later, on February 6th, 1870, a far heavier loss befell him: that of Mary, his wife. She had never been very robust, and had had more than one serious illness. For the last three years her strength had been visibly failing. Then, at the end of January, 1870, rheumatic fever developed, and after six days of great suffering, she died. She was 72.

George Müller's entry in his diary was: 'On October 7th, 1830, therefore 39 years and 4 months ago, the Lord gave me my most valuable, lovely and holy wife. Her value to me, and the blessing God made her to me, is beyond description. This blessing was continued to me till this day, when this afternoon, about four o'clock, the Lord took her to Himself.'

Then on February 11th, he wrote: 'To-day the earthly remains of my precious wife were laid in the grave. Many thousands of persons showed the deepest sympathy. About 1,400 of the orphans who were able to walk followed in the procession; the whole staff of Helpers at the Orphan Houses who could be spared, and hundreds of believers of the Church with which she had been in communion; I myself, sustained by the Lord to the utmost, performed the service at the chapel, in the cemetery, etc.

Shortly after the funeral I was unwell, but as soon as I was sufficiently recovered, I preached my late dear wife's funeral sermon.'

The sermon was afterwards published in the *Narrative*, and he prefaces it by saying: 'As all the principal matters connected with her illness, her removal, our happy conjugal life, and usefulness as a helper in the work of the Lord, are contained in the funeral sermon, I give it here; and also because the reader will thus be furnished somewhat better with the inner life and ways of the writer, than otherwise he would.'

Like all of George Müller's statements, this last one is perfectly accurate. But also, in attempting to understand this amazing man, his words and actions are seen to be consistent only if we take his statements literally. Everyone is only too accustomed to reading and listening to pious catch-phrases. Most of us are so determined not to be misled by superficial professions of faith, that we almost automatically discount such utterances and are on our guard with those who make them. Thus

114

when we read that George Müller not only conducted the service at his wife's funeral, but was able to bring himself to preach a long sermon about her without breaking down, we are perhaps all too ready to conclude that the lovely things he said about her cannot possibly ring true, and that he must have really been a cold-hearted individual. Even the information, given by a close friend, John Pocock, that when it was all over Müller sat down at the vestry table, buried his face in his hands, and did not move or speak for two hours, does not quite remove our suspicions. The truth seems to be, that on the natural plane George Müller was, like other bereaved husbands, dreadfully conscious of an aching void and terrible loneliness. But on the spiritual plane he was able truly to say and to feel, in the words of the text of his funeral sermon, 'Thou art good, and doest good.' That was the whole secret. Men and women, even those who are Christians, are, to a greater or lesser extent, rebels against God. Most of us have areas, or at least little pockets, in our souls where some degree of rebellion is going on. But George Müller had allowed the Holy Spirit to rid his soul of rebellion. He really was, in the most literal sense, *satisfied* with God. In his case it was not a question of saying, 'I shall be satisfied, when I awake, with Thy likeness.' He truly was satisfied with his Lord, here and now.

That is why he could take, with perfect sincerity, as the three headings of his sermon: i. The Lord was good, and did good, in giving her to me. ii. He was good, and did good, in so long leaving her to me. iii. He was good, and did good, in taking her from me.

The sermon is remarkable, and it is a pity that its length makes it impossible to quote it all. My own reactions to it were: on first reading, it slightly repelled me. I had not studied George Müller's character so closely then, and I judged it too much on natural levels; on second reading, a long time after the first, I began to revise my first impression; on third reading I was struck by the extraordinary beauty of the Müllers' married life; and on fourth, I began to apprehend the spiritual depths of the man who preached the sermon, and also those of the woman of whom he was speaking. I began to agree with him when he said, 'that at the departure of such a Christian, we should ponder the lessons which her life is calculated to teach.'

It is, however, essential to remember that George Müller was not an Englishman. I do not think that any Englishman, however devout, however affectionate, could have preached that sermon. The English are too inhibited in their emotions to make it possible for them to express themselves so unselfconsciously, or to reveal the secrets of their hearts in such a manner. It is

116

worthwhile to bear in mind that that sermon was given by a German, who, though dignified in his manner and conversation generally, was not hindered by that reserve which would make it impossible for an Englishman to express himself so unaffectedly and freely in such circumstances.

In the sermon he covers Mary Müller's whole life from their engagement to her death in great detail. He describes how he was led to meet her, to propose to her, and so on all through the rest of her life. He describes her excellent education, her accomplishments in playing the piano and painting, which she sacrificed, to give her time entirely to caring for the orphans. 'My beloved wife could do fancy needlework as other ladies, and had done it when young, but she did not thus occupy her time, except she would with her own dear hands now and then net a purse for her husband when she was in the country for change of air. Her occupation had habitually a useful end. It was to get ready the many hundreds of neat little beds for the dear orphans, most of whom had never seen such beds, far less slept in them, that she laboured. It was to provide numberless other useful things in the Orphan Houses, and especially in the sick rooms of the orphans, that, day by day, except on the Lord's Day, she was seen in the Orphan Houses.'

He describes their happiness in each other. 'I

never saw my beloved wife at any time, without being delighted so to do. Thousands of times I told her—"My darling, I never saw you at any time since you became my wife, without my being delighted to see you."' He describes how he would sit by her side for half an hour, while she rested each afternoon, after an illness in 1860. 'I knew that it was good for her that her dear, active mind and hands should have rest, and I knew well that this would not be, except her husband was by her side; moreover I also needed a little rest, on account of my weak digestive powers: and therefore I spent these precious moments with my darling wife. There we sat, side by side, her hand in mine, as an habitual thing, having a few words of loving intercourse, or being silent, but most happy in the Lord, and in each other.'

He speaks of their prayer times. Every day, in addition to their own private prayers and family prayers, they met together two or three times for prayer together. In the evening, during their last hour at the Orphan Houses before going home to bed, she would come to his room, and they would pray together. 'Our prayer, and supplication, and intercession, mingled with thanksgiving, lasted generally forty minutes, fifty minutes and sometimes the whole hour. At these seasons we brought perhaps fifty or more points, or persons, or circumstances, before God ... I judge that it was in our own history the great secret for the continuation not only of conjugal happiness, but of the love to each other, which was even more abundantly fresh and warm than it had been during the first year, though we were *then* exceedingly fond of each other.'

Towards the end of the sermon he says, 'Knowing, as I do, the deep personal attachment that my dearest wife had to that Blessed One who hung for us on the Cross, can it be otherwise than that my inmost soul should rejoice in the joy which my loved one has now, in being with the Lord Jesus for ever? The depth of my love for her is rejoicing in her joy. As a husband, I feel more and more every day that I am without this pleasant, useful, loving companion. As the Director of the Orphan Houses, I miss her in numberless ways and shall miss her yet more and more. But as a child of God, and as the servant of the Lord Jesus, I bow, I am satisfied with the will of my Heavenly Father, I seek by perfect submission to His holy will to glorify Him, I kiss continually the hand that has thus afflicted me; but I also say, I shall meet her again, to spend a happy eternity with her.'

As a footnote to the sermon, he afterwards added: 'When now, between eight and nine o'clock in the evenings I went home from the Orphan Houses, instead of in company with my beloved wife, as for so many years past (for she

119

was always with me), I said to myself, "I shall not meet my beloved wife at home, but I shall meet the Lord Jesus, my precious Friend; He will comfort me;" and I thanked God that He had left to me my beloved daughter, who always watched for my arrival, to greet me, and did all she could to soothe my bereaved heart. But the loss was great, the wound was deep, and as weeks and months passed on, while continuing *habitually* not only to be satisfied with God, but also to praise Him, for what He had done in thus bereaving me, the wound seemed to deepen instead of being healed, and the bereavement to be felt more and more.'

The entries in the *Autobiography* for the years 1871 and 1872 record three events only, but three which are closely connected. They are, Lydia Müller's marriage to James Wright, George Müller's own second marriage, and the appointment of James Wright to be co-director.

James Wright had been known to George Müller for thirty years; in fact, since boyhood. He was his principal helper in the work of the Scriptural Knowledge Institution, and by all accounts a saintly man. He was an able worker, an excellent preacher and conscientious to a degree in carrying on the work according to the principles which Müller laid down. A scrupulous determination to ensure that Müller's oft-repeated behests that no veneration should be paid to George Müller led him, after his father-in-law's death, to destroy the original manuscript of the *Narrative*; a piece of well-meant vandalism that it is useless to lament, but which succeeding generations will surely regret more and more.

Wright had been married before, and cannot have been a widower longer than a year or two when in August, 1871, he asked Mr. Müller for his daughter's hand. This offer from Wright came as a complete surprise to him, though to the reader a proposal from such a quarter to the daughter of George Müller seems just what one might expect. Lydia was probably less astonished than her father, and nothing loth, except that she could not bear the thought of leaving him alone so soon after her mother's death. He tells how that she was in a great conflict of mind about it for a whole fortnight, and it was not until he begged her not to let such a thought stand in her way, and that it would be such a joy and comfort to see her married to such a man, that she accepted James Wright's offer. They were married on November 16th of that same year, when Lydia was thirty-nine.

In May, 1872, Wright was officially appointed Müller's co-director of the Institution, and his successor in the event of his death. Müller laid great stress on the fact that he had chosen Wright, not because he was his son-in-law, but because he considered him to be the ideal man for the position. He tells how he had first broached the subject to him before, during the lifetime of Wright's first wife. Both George and Mary Müller had a great regard for him who had always been one of their most valuable helpers, and for nearly ten years they prayed that God would fit him to become Müller's successor. It was a long time before Wright was prepared to accept such responsibilities, feeling himself quite unworthy of them. Also his first wife, then still alive and in her usual health, thought he would be overburdening himself. But Mrs. Wright, who Müller describes as 'his excellent Christian wife', soon gave way, convinced that it was God's will for her husband. Wright himself, after much hesitation, came to the conclusion that he should no longer refuse Müller's offer.

Müller wrote, 'By the Lord's kindness I am able to work as heretofore, I may say with little hindrance through illness; yet I cannot conceal from myself that it is of great importance for the work that I should obtain a measure of relief. This relief, however, can be really only given to me by one who stands in a similar position to the work, and who, when I am away, or when I may feel it desirable to have a real rest, could do all I ordinarily do in directing. On this account, therefore, I not only appointed Mr. Wright as my successor, in the event of my death, but from May 26th, 1872, associated him also with me in the direction of the Institution, which year by year increases in extent; and I cannot describe my joy, in having found in him a successor in the event of my death.'

George Müller had lived so long under the same roof as women who were devoted to him and he to them, his wife and his daughter, that the prospect of being quite alone was intolerable. His second entry into matrimony is given thus in the *Narrative*:

'The engagement of my beloved daughter, together with a variety of reasons, finally led me to the decision to marry again; as not only from the time of my bereavement I greatly missed my beloved departed wife, in my position, but judged, that now, in the prospect of my beloved daughter's marriage it would be best for me. This decision, as one of the deepest importance, was come to in the fear of God, and in the full assurance that I had the sanction and approval of my Heavenly Father. I married on November 30th, 1871, Miss Susannah Grace Sangar, whom I had known for twenty-five years as a consistent Christian, and regarding whom I had every reason to believe that she would prove a helper to me in my various services.'

CHAPTER TEN

THE PREACHING TOURS

Susannah Sangar was in her late forties at the time of her marriage to George Müller. She had been a governess in a family in Clifton. It is hard to assess the success or otherwise of this marriage. Müller speaks of her with respect and affection in his *Narrative*, never referring to her except as 'my dear wife' and never giving the slightest hint that the marriage was anything but a blessing to him. But it seems certain, from what has filtered down to our time from those who were personally acquainted with them both, that their natures did not dovetail as his and Mary's had done. Susannah was undoubtedly devoted to her husband, but she does not seem to have been an entirely easy person with whom to get on, nor to have been able to bring herself to take up the work among the orphans as had her predecessor. Müller makes no mention of this, but no doubt made it a matter of urgent prayer, and a way out of the impasse was soon shown to him. Susannah Müller loved travel, and her husband perceived in this the solution to the problem. Travel would bring relief to her nervous state, and at the same time provide him with the opportunity that he had, in a sense, longed for all his life, to go to foreign lands and preach the Gospel. Had he attempted to do this as a young man he would probably have made little impression upon his hearers, as he was not especially gifted as a preacher. But he had always waited to know God's will, and His guidance had always pointed to his staying in Bristol, organizing the Scriptural Knowledge Institution, setting up the Orphan Houses, and ministering at Bethesda and Gideon chapels. Now the situation was different. He could leave the orphans and the other work in charge of his co-director James Wright, his son-in-law. Now, at the age of seventy, his name and work known throughout the world, he was assured of an eager and attentive audience wherever he went.

Susannah was the ideal companion for him on such an enterprise. She was entirely fitted to be the wife of a travelling missionary, and was undaunted by heat, cold or the vicissitudes of travel in outlandish places. She never appeared on any platform herself, but took a definite part in what in present-day evangelistic crusades is known as 'counselling'. She also wrote numbers of letters for her husband, and seems to have been a kind of secretary and nurse-companion combined. Müller's health in old age was very good, and he was an excellent traveller, but youthful in body and spirit though he was, at his age he could never have embarked on such adventures in unknown and far-flung places without someone much younger than himself to care for him. His wife was well able to do this, and on at least one occasion, when he was near to death from heat-exhaustion, saved his life by her intelligent and energetic dealing with the situation. She had plenty of ideas, too, and even wrote two books, now out of print, though copies are still in existence. One was called *The Life and Labours of George Müller*, which gives the substances of the *Narrative* in a very abbreviated form. The other, *The Preaching Tours and Missionary Labours of George Müller*, is a longer book, written in the first person plural, as it relates to her experiences as well as his. This book is not without plenty of caustic comments on the error, idolatry and general inefficiency encountered in benighted places.

Here, in brief outline, are George Müller's preaching tours

First Tour: March 26th to July 6th, 1875. England: Brighton, London, Sunderland, Newcastle. Müller preached at the Mildmay Conference three times, to 3,000 hearers each time; at the Metropolitan Tabernacle, by Spurgeon's invitation; and to 1,500 Christian workers at the 'Edinburgh Castle' in the East End of London, which was Dr. Barnardo's centre of evangelism. On this tour he preached seventy times in all.

Second Tour: August 14th, 1875, to July 5th, 1876. England, Scotland and Ireland. He addressed some huge meetings on this tour, and probably the largest were those at Victoria Hall in Liverpool, which had been built for Moody and Sankey's missions. On Sundays, during his five weeks' stay, he generally had an audience of 5,000 or 6,000 on both Sunday afternoons and Sunday evenings, and 2,000 to 2,500 twice each week-day. At the very first of the meetings in this hall one of his old orphans, the commander of a large merchant vessel, was converted.

Third Tour: August 16th, 1876 to June 25th, 1877. Switzerland, Germany and Holland. Altogether he preached 302 times in sixty-eight places, most of which were large towns. On his foreign tours he usually preached in English or in German; sometimes in French. Where none of these languages was understood, he would have an interpreter. As a rest from the strain of constant preaching, he, with his wife, did a good deal of sightseeing as they travelled, sometimes taking a few days especially for the purpose. They even embarked on such adventures as ascending the Rigi in the Alps by cog-wheel railway, passing the night in a hotel, and awaking at 4 a.m. to see the sunrise on the mountain top. A few days later they passed a very cold night in a bedroom without a fire in the Hospice at the top of the St. Gothard Pass, 9,000 feet above sea level. They do not seem to have come to any harm, however, and Müller fulfilled all his preaching engagements.

Fourth Tour: Canada and the United States. August 18th, 1877, to July 8th, 1878. The Müllers travelled more than 19,000 miles by land and water on this tour, and he preached 299 times. They had many interesting experiences, including a visit to the White House, where they were introduced to President and Mrs. Hayes who received them with much courtesy. The President had half an hour's conversation with Mr. Müller, and afterwards Mrs. Hayes herself took them over the White House and showed them the State Apartments. In her account of this tour, Mrs. Müller thus describes another encounter. 'At London, Ontario, we were introduced to the Reverend Josiah Henson, a venerable negro with a pleasant expression of countenance and white hair, who shook hands with us most cordially. This was "Uncle Tom", the hero of *Uncle Tom's Cabin*.' She means his prototype, of course, as 'Uncle Tom' is a fictional character. Many of Harriet Beecher Stowe's characters were drawn at least partly from life.

George Müller's fame had preceded him everywhere in the States and in Canada, and he was invited by the Presidents and Professors of fifteen universities to address the students. He visited churches, chapels, schools, colleges, orphanages and institutions of every kind. At

Dr. Cullis's Institution for Consumptive Patients, its Founder told Müller, 'But for your example all this would never have been in existence.'

Here are the chief places he visited, addressing great congregations, some white, some coloured: New York, Boston, Jersey City, Philadelphia, Baltimore, Washington, Columbia, S.C., Charleston, Savannah, Jacksonville, Florida, New Orleans—from whence they travelled 800 miles up the Mississippi to Memphis; St Louis, Sherman—8,235 feet above sea level, which has the highest railway station in the world. The cold there was intense. The railway crossed prairies, the alkali desert and the Sierra Nevada Mountains into California; Sacramento, San Francisco—which the Müllers reached after six days and five nights spent continuously in the train from St. Louis; Santa Cruz—where they saw the giant redwoods; Stockton—where the heat was tremendous.

Nor was the heat the worst trial. Mrs. Müller writes: 'There, too, at night, we had a terrible conflict with the mosquitoes; but although we killed them by the score, could do very little in the way of exterminating the foe, so that our visit to Stockton was marked by a regular mosquito war. Our rest at night was so disturbed that we were scarcely fit for travelling, but having been repeatedly advised by several Christian friends on no account to leave California without visiting the Yosemite Valley in that State, and as my husband desired to have a little break for a few days, after so much constant preaching, on May 24th, at 8 a.m. we left by train for Milton, thirty miles from Stockton.' She then describes their adventures on this trip. They travelled, after leaving Milton by Californian stage-waggon, with a coachman who drove furiously. They were so terrifically jolted that they were thankful to reach the end of the stage without broken bones. They reached a hotel after 11½ hours of continuous travelling, and at least there was not one mosquito to keep them awake. Next day they set off again with another driver, who took them along at a reasonable pace. They travelled all day until 4 p.m. After passing the summit of the hill they had been ascending all day, 8,000 feet above sea level, they began to move down into the Yosemite Valley, magnificent scenery of rocks and cliffs and waterfalls meeting them at every turn. They reached the hotel at 6 p.m. Next day, which was Sunday, Müller preached in the dining-room to visitors to that hotel, and two others in the valley, who had gathered to hear him. The Müllers spent three days in the wonderful valley, and started on their return journey on May 29th.

A strange incident occurred as they were in

the stage-waggon on a mountain road. A cart approached them, in which were a man and woman. The cart drew to one side to let the coach pass, when just as the two vehicles were abreast of each other the woman in the cart stood up and eagerly called out: 'Is that George Müller?' He replied, 'It is'. 'Then I *must* shake hands with you, sir. I have read your *Life of Trust*, and it has been a great blessing to my soul.' She leaned forward and held out her hand, and the Müllers shook hands with her and with her husband, having no idea who she was or where she came from, and there was no time to ask. Her last words were, 'Pray for me.' On May 30th, the Müllers reached Milton once more, and by telegraphing for their luggage were able to have it sent on, so that there was no need to return to Stockton and the mosquitoes. The Yosemite holiday, which really was a journey into the unknown by primitive transport, with the quality of the accommodation on route uncertain in the extreme, does show that the two were game for anything, in spite of George Müller's seventy-four years.

They went on to Salt Lake City, where he preached in the Congregationalist and Methodist churches, and many Mormons came to the meetings. The Müllers visited the Mormon Tabernacle, which was said to hold 13,000 people; Mrs. Müller wrote that she doubted whether it could possibly hold more than 10,000. Had she uttered the words aloud one feels that her accents would have been scathing. She did not approve of Mormons!

The Müllers continued their tour to Omaha, Chicago, Cleveland, Gettysburg; then back to New York from whence they sailed for England.

During their stay in the States they met several people who had been orphans at Ashley Down, and these had welcomed them with great pleasure. On their return to Bristol they had an equally warm welcome from the present orphans. 'At 3 p.m. we landed at Liverpool, returning the following day to Bristol, and upon arriving in an open carriage at the top of Ashley Hill at half past four, found a little army of the orphan boys and girls, with almost all our helpers at the Orphan Houses, waiting to receive us. There, as we drove slowly along, the boys cheered heartily, and the girls waved their handkerchiefs, determined (as a bystander remarked) to give us "a right royal welcome"; and at the entrance of New Orphan House Number 3, a crowd of children closed round us, with loving, friendly greetings.' So Mrs. Müller finishes her account of the first American Tour.

Fifth Tour: Switzerland, France, Spain and Italy. September 5th, 1878 to June 18th, 1879. While in Spain, George Müller was able to visit for the first time the ten Day Schools in

Barcelona, and the five in Madrid, which were supported by the Scriptural Knowledge Institution. At Mentone he had several conversations with Spurgeon, whose stay there happened to coincide with his own.

Sixth Tour: United States and Canada. August 27th, 1879, to June 17th, 1880. Müller preached 299 times in 42 places. On this trip he preached many times to Germans in their own language. He stated that there were nine million Germans in the U.S.A. at that time.

Seventh Tour: Canada and the United States, September 15th, 1880 to May 31st, 1881. Having left America with 154 written invitations to preach which he had not been able to accept for lack of time, he decided to return only two months later. Particularly he felt called to preach to the Germans there, as thousands of immigrants were pouring into the States from Germany and Switzerland. In New York alone he preached, during this tour, 38 times in German and 54 in English. He visited Yale, and addressed a large number of students, 'a service in which I take the deepest interest, from having been converted myself while a student at the University of Halle.'

Eighth Tour: Egypt, Palestine, Syria, Asia Minor, Turkey and Greece. August 23rd, 1881, to May 30th, 1882. This tour demonstrated the enterprise and daring of the Müllers, as their journeyings were accompanied by hardships that would have daunted many people half their age. The ship could not come into harbour at Jaffa, so that the landing had to be by a boat, rowed by eight Arabs, in a very rough sea and through tremendous surf. They journeyed to Jerusalem from Jaffa along the only made road in Palestine, which Müller describes as worse than the worst of the many bad roads on which they had travelled in Europe. In Jerusalem itself, no vehicle could enter the city, owing to the narrowness and badly-paved state of the streets. In spite of these difficulties, the Müllers visited Bethany, the Mount of Olives, the Garden of Gethsemane, the Pool of Bethesda, the Mosque of Omar (where the Temple once stood) and the Church of the Holy Sepulchre. During his stay in Jerusalem Müller preached many times in English and German, sometimes with translation into Arabic.

While in Egypt they visited the Pyramids and the Sphinx, and he preached several times in both Cairo and Alexandria.

Ninth Tour: Germany, Austria, Hungary, Bohemia, Russia and Poland. August 8th, 1882 to June 1st, 1883. The chief hindrances to his missionary efforts which stand out in Müller's account of this tour is the lack of religious liberty in some of the countries visited, particularly in Austria and Russia. In St. Petersburg he was warmly received by Colonel Paschkoff and Princess Lieven, both of whom had been converted by Lord Radstock on one of his evangelistic visits to the Russian capital a few years before. The Princess was so anxious that the Müllers should stay at her house that George Müller for once broke his usual rule of staying at hotels rather than with friends. (He found that he had more time for rest and prayer in a hotel.) He and his wife were entertained with great kindness at her mansion for nearly eleven weeks.

He was able to preach in English in the British and American Chapel without a permit, as it had no connection with the State. He was able to obtain permission, through Russian friends, to preach at the German churches in St. Petersburg, and also to the Swedes, with an interpreter, in the British Chapel. Not knowing any Russian, he was not very clear as to what was covered by his permit, and held some drawing-room meetings in Colonel Paschkoff's house. This soon resulted in a summons to appear before the Director of Police, who told him that he had gone beyond his permit. The meetings in Paschkoff's house had to be abandoned. Paschkoff himself was constantly harried and persecuted on account of his evangelistic zeal. At one period the meetings in his house had been attended regularly by more than a thousand people, but at the time of Müller's visit not more than twenty were allowed to be gathered at any meeting.

Paschkoff had been banished from his country house near Moscow because he had expounded the Bible to the poor. He was a personal friend of the Tzar, who was not himself antagonistic to the Evangelical Movement, and would have preferred to protect it. But government officials, frightened of anything that seemed likely to undermine the autocracy, brought such powerful persuasion to bear upon the Tzar that he gave way and outlawed the movement. Many people of high rank, including Paschkoff, were eventually banished to their estates or exiled from the country, and lesser men were sent to Siberia. Thus the Russian government of the day in its blindness, and the Tzar in his weakness, by suppressing the Evangelical Movement threw out that which would almost certainly have purified Russian life and given entrance to liberal ideas, and quite probably have spared the world the results of the Revolution of 1917. Considering all that has happened in Russia since George Müller's visit, there is something rather impressive about the following short entry in the 117th Annual Report of the Müller Homes, published in 1956, quoted from a letter received at the Homes. (Possibly 'Moscow' should read 'Leningrad'. There is no record of Müller's ever having gone to Moscow.)

'I was very interested to read in —— that the Russian Delegation to the World Congress, recently held in London, made a pilgrimage to Bristol to stand beside Mr. Müller's grave. He preached once in Moscow, and I thought it a fine testimony to the impression that he must have made that he is still held in reverence.'

Tenth Tour: India. September 26th, 1883, to June 5th, 1884. In his youth Müller had wanted to go to India, and tells that four times in the eight years following his conversion, he offered himself to God for such a service, but the more he prayed, the more it seemed manifest that he should remain in England. Now, at the age of seventy-eight, he felt that the call had come at last. He travelled all over India, and preached everywhere he went, in spite of the heat and other discomforts. He and his wife journeyed twenty-one thousand miles on this tour, and he preached 206 times. His comment on the Himalayas is worth quoting. 'On the fifth day of our stay at Darjeeling the sky was clear enough for us to see the highest mountain range in the world, which is perpetually covered in snow. The amazing grandeur and magnificence of this mountain range will never be erased from the mind of any God-fearing person who has seen it.'

He preached at Colombo, Madras, Calcutta, Darjeeling, Benares, Cawnpore, Agra, Lahore, Delhi, Poona, Bombay and several other places. Mrs. Müller writes graphically of what they saw, and the emotions thus caused. She describes their feelings when standing in places which recalled scenes of the Indian Mutiny with all its horrors: their surprise and regret on learning that the British Government did not permit the 1,600 prisoners in Lahore gaol to receive Christian teaching from the missionaries; the sense of oppression caused by the sight of the idolatory at Benares which surpassed anything they had seen in all their travels. She writes that although both of them had been reading and hearing about missionaries and mission work all their lives, 'We never really realized, until we visited Benares, the awful conditions in which the heathens live and die.' The things she saw on this tour so moved her that she closes her chapter with a most urgent exhortation to Christian people to leave the comforts of life in England and go out, if possible, as missionaries, or, if they could not do so, to give their money freely.

Eleventh Tour: England and South Wales. August 18th to October 2nd, 1884. This tour was cut short because Mrs. Müller was attacked by erysipelas while in Pembrokeshire, and the doctor who was called in advised them to return home at once, which they did.

Twelfth Tour: England. May 16th to July 1st, 1885. Like the previous tour, this one was cut short by illness. This time it was George Müller who was ill. He caught a violent cold at

Wellington in Shropshire, and was so poorly that his wife persuaded him to give up their proposed visit to Ireland, and go to the Isle of Wight for a rest; eventually they went home to Bristol.

Thirteenth Tour: England and Scotland. September 1st to October 3rd, 1885. This brief tour took them to Liverpool and Dundee, in each of which places George Müller preached several times.

Fourteenth Tour: Australia, China, Japan and the Straits of Malacca. November 4th, 1885, to June 13th, 1887. George Müller began his missionary efforts on this tour with preaching engagements in New York, lasting three weeks. Then the Müllers crossed the American continent by rail, and sailed for Australia from San Francisco. Müller preached at Sydney, Melbourne, Brisbane; sailed from Brisbane for Java, but could not preach there because no able interpreter could be found; went on to Hong Kong, Shanghai, Hankow, and Chinkiang; returned to Shanghai, and sailed for Japan, landing at Nagasaki; preached at Yokohama, Tokio, Kobe, Osaka and Kioto, with interpreters; returned to Hong Kong, where a severe cold prevented him holding any meetings; went to Singapore, Penang, Colombo, and from thence home via Marseilles and Nice. The Müllers travelled 37,280 miles on this tour.

Fifteenth Tour: Australia, Tasmania, New Zealand, Ceylon and India. August 10th, 1887, to March 11th, 1890. This visit to Australia started on the west coast, at Albany, from where they went on to Adelaide and fifteen other towns, Müller preaching six and sometimes seven times every week to crowded audiences. Then from Melbourne, he and his wife sailed for Tasmania, where he preached twenty-five times. On February 23rd they sailed for New Zealand, where he preached many times in and around Wellington and Auckland. Then back to Sydney, then to Ceylon, on to Calcutta and from there to Darjeeling, whence they were driven by the intense heat in Calcutta. It was on this journey that George Müller was so overcome by heat exhaustion in the train that Mrs. Müller feared he was going to die. She thus describes the ordeal. 'On April 29th we left Calcutta by the 4.30 p.m. train; but soon after our departure from the railway station, my beloved husband—though an excellent traveller, and one among a thousand in his ability to endure fatigue—became so extremely unwell from exhaustion, produced by the amazing heat, that I was exceedingly alarmed, and feared that he might die suddenly in the train. I knew, too, that there were no hotels on the road, nor any railway stations at which we could stop with anything like comfort; so I persuaded him to lie down upon one of the long

140

seats of the saloon compartment we occupied, in which, happily, there were no other passengers besides ourselves; placed one of the pillows we carry with us, when taking night journeys, under his head, and kept all the windows open so that we might not lose a single breath of air. I fanned him repeatedly also with a large fan, persuaded him to drink a little of the wine and water, and to eat a few of the sandwiches we had with us, and begged him, if possible, to try and sleep. When the train stopped long enough at the stations, too, and Nathaniel (the native servant who travelled with them) came to ask us if we wanted anything, I sent him to fetch a cup of tea for Mr. Müller, or a glass of lemonade; and in answer to repeated, fervent prayer, managed to keep life in him until we arrived at Damookdea Ghat, where we arrived at nine in the evening. There, finding his pulse was good, I took courage; we went on board the ferry-steamer immediately, where, seated upon a chair on the deck, he found the breezes blowing over the Ganges exceedingly refreshing; and at Sara Ghat, we went on shore.' They went on to Darjeeling, and, says his wife, 'There, in a few days, Mr. Müller regained his ordinary good health, and I am thankful to say that through the Lord's kindness, he became as well and strong as usual.' And George Müller was eighty-three, and had been so delicate in his youth! But it is the wife, almost more than the husband, who arrests one's attention in this episode. She may not have been 'easy'; she had her faults, no doubt; but what courage, what resourcefulness, and what selfless devotion she showed on this occasion! In that gruelling heat she was probably suffering little less than he was, but all her thought seemed to have been how to bring relief to him.

From Darjeeling they went on to Simla, Delhi, Agra, Cawnpore, Allahabad, Jubbulpore. There a heavy blow fell. George Müller writes: 'While thus quietly and happily going on in my service at Jubbulpore, a letter was handed to me from a missionary at Agra, to whom Mr. Wright had sent a telegram, that he might inform me of the death of my beloved daughter, his wife. Our plans were now completely altered, and it was obvious, after prayer, that we ought as soon as possible to return to England, and see what could be done to fill up the place of my dear daughter, who for nearly thirty years had gratuitously laboured at the Orphan Houses, but who died in Bristol on January 10th, 1890, in the 58th year of her age.'

Mrs. Müller's book about the preaching tours finishes in the middle of this tour, while they were still at Simla, and it is worth quoting her final paragraph, which reveals the woman herself, and speaks of an earnest and devoted nature. 'I desire now to close this record of our travels, by expressing our deep gratitude to the Lord, for all His many mercies to us, in the course of these extensive missionary tours. Times without number we have been shielded from danger; during our long journeys by railway, no accidents have befallen us, and though many times tossed about on board ship upon the ocean, during storms and tempests, we have never been shipwrecked, nor have we really *suffered* from these long voyages in the least. Many of these blessings, I doubt not, we owe to the prayers of Christian friends, whose supplications on our behalf I would therefore earnestly ask them to continue. I would also remind the believing reader of the foregoing pages, that we have but "one brief life", that we know not how soon our earthly pilgrimage may end, and that we should seek, *with all earnestness*, to devote that "one brief life" to God; and should this book be directed into the hands of unconverted persons, to such I would say, ask the Lord to show you, by His Spirit, that you are lost, ruined and undone; put your trust in the Lord Jesus Christ alone, for pardon and salvation; and seek to live *only* for Him. Time is short; delay is dangerous; and the stupendous realities of the eternal world will soon break in upon us. Dear reader, where will you spend eternity?'

Sixteenth Tour: Germany, Switzerland. August 8th, 1890 to June 5th, 1891. George Müller was now eighty-four, and one would imagine that touring in other lands would have been too much strain at his age. But this was not at all the case, by his own showing. He opens his own account of this tour by saying that, following his return from India, he worked at the Orphan Houses for four months and then, finding himself 'in much need of rest,' he and his wife left home again on this, their sixteenth tour.

He held numerous meetings at Heidelberg, Stuttgart, Schaffhausen, Zurich, Basel, Barne, Thun, Langnau, St. Gallen, Constance, Carlsruhe, Pforzheim, Freiburg, Wiesbaden, Frankfort-on-Main, Bonn, Essen, Eberfield.

His congregations on this tour were very large, and at Pforzheim he had difficulty in pressing through the crowd to the desk from which he was to preach, and for the final services had to be admitted by a side door. At Langnau, where the Müllers stayed in November, the cold was intense, the temperature falling to twelve degrees. Having spent so much time in the tropics, and only the previous year experienced the intensity of the hot season in India, they felt the cold very much, but even so do not seem to have been incapacitated by it.

Seventeenth Tour: Germany, Austria and Italy. June, 1891 to May, 1892. This tour was really an extension of the previous one, as they did not return to England in between. George Müller preached in Cassel, Berlin, Hamburg, Halberstadt, Heimersleben, Magdeburg, Brandenburg, Stettin, Breslau, Vienna, Florence, Naples. From Naples they returned home after an absence of a year and nine months.

He records that in the seventeen years of his tours, he and his wife travelled 200,000 miles.

Writing in the *Report* for 1888, George Müller described some of the acute discomforts which he and his wife had experienced over the years. He wrote this paragraph after one of his visits to India. They had worked in Calcutta for fifteen weeks, until the thermometer stood at 115° in the shade, and neither of them could endure the overwhelming heat any longer, and so they had gone away for a time to Darjeeling in the Himalayas.

'During *some* of my Tours, we have for many weeks together been exposed to cold from fifty to fifty-six degrees below freezing point; and at other times to heat from ninety to one hundred and ten and upwards, discomforts which must have been experienced to know the full force of them. Then, on the sea, again and again, very heavy gales, and even a typhoon, have overtaken us, when the trials thus occasioned were severe. On the land we have had to travel, on a stretch, not merely for twenty or thirty hours uninterruptedly, but more than once we have been on the railway six days and six nights in succession. Though, on the whole, we have had excellent accommodation during our long journeys, yet *sometimes* we have been *obliged* to put up with the most *trying* and *inferior* kind. Twice, though in the best cabins, on board large, first-class steam-ships, we have been exceedingly tried by *insects*; in the United States, in New South Wales, in Ceylon and in India, the mosquitoes were *most grievous*; and in two first-class steamships, *rats* so abounded that they ran over us by night. Yet hitherto God has helped us, and, we doubt not, *will* help us to the end.'

Towards the end of the fourth volume of the *Narrative*, published in 1886, Müller finished his account of his preaching tour on the Continent in 1876-7 by emphasizing that it had had no connection with the Scriptural Knowledge Institution. He says, 'It was not undertaken for the purpose of collecting money for it, nor even for the purpose of bringing it before my hearers on the Continent; but solely that by my experience and knowledge in divine things I might benefit Christians and especially younger believers, and that I might preach the Gospel to the unconverted. I did not even refer to the Institution, except when especially requested to do so.' Presumably all of this applied to his other tours also.

A question which naturally arises in the mind is: Who paid for these tours. Page 29 in Volume

IV of the *Narrative* supplies the answer. In his usual candid way Müller sets it all out thus: 'August 23rd, 1877. During the past three years and three months, whilst almost constantly moving about from city to city and country to country, in connection with my preaching tours, the Lord was pleased, as during 45 years previously, to supply all my need; so that while I was travelling about for 14½ months in England, Scotland and Ireland, with my dear wife, at a very heavy expense, God helped us. Afterwards I was 10½ months labouring in the work in Switzerland, the German Empire and the Kingdom of Holland, when the expenses were still greater; yet again God bountifully supplied me.' Then he describes what happened when he and his wife went to America. 'The passage money and extra preparations for that country took a considerable sum, but God supplied all. Then, on our arrival in the United States, we had to travel many thousands of miles and to live in hotels at a very heavy expense, but God supplied all our need; and after all was accomplished, though our return to Europe required the expenditure of a considerable sum, yet we lacked nothing. And thus, with the prospect before of spending the evening of my life in going from country to country, and of having to meet all the heavy expenses of this mode of life, which are three times greater than our former housekeeping, I find it unspeakably blessed to have my Father in Heaven to go to for the supply of all my wants; for I am sure that He will never leave me nor forsake me.'

He always expected to pay fares and hotel bills out of the money which had been sent for his own use in answer to prayer, rather than look for hospitality from Christian people encountered in the course of his travels. When, as occasionally happened, someone en route insisted on paying his hotel bill, he would refer to it specifically when next writing on the subject, recording the value of contributions made in this way separately from those that came in other ways.

A definite statement about the manner in which the tours were financed appears on the final page of the *Narrative*, thus: He writes that in the twelve years from 1874 to 1885 he and his wife had received £30,000 in gifts for their personal use, of which they had given away more than £27,000. 'To this last sum is to be added the many hundreds of pounds, spent out of my own means, in connection with our missionary tours.'

Almost the last words of Volume IV of the *Narrative* are these: 'You will see, esteemed reader, from what has gone before, the result of systematic giving; but of the joy of God, and the blessing received in my own soul, I can give you no description whatever.'

CHAPTER ELEVEN

THE PASSING OF GEORGE MÜLLER

January 13th, 1894. 'Today it pleased God to take to Himself my beloved wife, after He had left her to me twenty-three years and six months.' Thus George Müller recorded the death of his second wife. He himself was now eighty-nine, and he looked back over the years of his two marriages, 'sixty-two years of happy married life,' as he described it, to see the hand of God in it all. When his first wife, his darling Mary, was taken from him, he tells how he was able to accept it in faith that as it came, as he absolutely believed, from God, so it must work out for his good. This remained a matter of faith for ten years, until suddenly one day, in the midst of his journeyings, the thought flashed upon him that had Mary lived, he could never have undertaken the missionary tours, because she would have been too old and too delicate for such arduous travelling, and at his age he could not have gone alone. It was his having a second wife who was only fifty-three when they began their travels that made them possible. Those world-wide evangelistic tours, which had given him the opportunity to witness for his Lord to thousands of people of all races, he counted among the most valuable work that God had permitted him to do.

But now Susannah too was gone, and he was left with neither wife nor daughter. He wrote, 'I continually praise God for what He gave me, for what He left me for a long time, and for what He has now taken; for it is all good for me. By constantly admiring the Lord's kindness to me in this very thing, that He has now entirely freed my beloved departed one from all bodily and spiritual infirmities and made her unspeakably happy in His presence, He overpowers my loneliness, and is doing more than merely supporting me. The dear departed one desired health to be able to labour for the dear orphans; for she loved her work among them greatly; she is now eternally free from all physical ailments, but for other service. She told me again and again, how she had thousands of times within the last ten years asked the Lord to fill her with His Spirit; she is now completely conformed to the mind of Christ, and unspeakably happy in His presence, and will be so eternally. This counterbalances not merely the feeling of great loneliness, in my case, but I praise God every day for what He has done, and I would not have it otherwise, for I really loved my dear departed one, and therefore rejoice in her present unspeakable happiness. I have written this because I consider it to be my special service to comfort tried ones, and to seek to strengthen the faith of the children of God.'

After his second wife's death, George Müller lived at Orphan House No. 3. He had always had his study there, and this study, though used by his successors, remained virtually unchanged for sixty years after his death. I myself was in it on an afternoon in May, 1958, less than a month before No. 3 House, the last of the Ashley Down Orphan Houses to be used for its original purpose, was given up, and the administration offices moved to 7 Cotham Park, Bristol. Mr. J. J. Rose, the present Director, sat at Mr. Müller's desk while we talked. The room itself was quite small, and the furniture solid and Victorian; the desk large and flat-topped, with several drawers. It was a perfectly ordinary study to look at, typical of hundreds of that period but with what wonderful associations to those who knew anything of its first occupant. What fervent prayers had been offered in that room, and what astounding answers to them had been received there; astounding to the ordinary mortal, but not to George Müller who expected them. What manifold contacts had taken place within those walls; discussions with celebrities such as Dr. Barnardo, Charles Dickens and Charles Haddon Spurgeon; conversations with obscure and humble Christians, who came to offer to Müller their gifts for God's work;

151

interviews with grandparents and other relatives who came to leave children in Müller's care, often placing an orphaned baby in his arms; partings with orphans about to venture forth into the world outside the Homes; those evening prayer periods with his wife Mary, when they met in this room evening by evening to bring every problem and every need to God before they went home to bed.

George Müller lived for another four years after Susannah's death. On his ninetieth birthday, in acknowledging a presentation made to him at Bethesda Chapel, he remarked that his voice was stronger than it had been sixty-nine year earlier, and that his mental powers were as good as ever. He was also still as quick in his movements as a young man, and he had no rheumatism. It will be remembered that as a young preacher he had been perpetually in the grip of one ailment or another; caused, at least partly, by the strain which he had thrown on his system by the reckless life he had lived before his conversion. But seventy years passed in perfect trust upon God, inwardly at peace whatever the outward circumstances, had swept the conflicts from his soul and the tension from his system, and his body at last expressed the health of his whole personality. His mental powers and his physical health continued right to the end.

Not long before he died, a friend said to him:

'When God calls you home, beloved Mr. Müller, it will be like a ship going into harbour full sail.' Müller instantly replied, 'Oh, no, it is poor George Müller, who needs daily to pray, "Hold Thou me up that my footsteps slip not."'

He preached his last sermon on the morning of Sunday, March 6th, 1898, at Alma Road Chapel, in Clifton. His subject was, 'Isaiah's Vision.' He worked as usual on Monday, Tuesday and Wednesday of that week, though on Wednesday he admitted to his son-in-law that he had felt weak while dressing that morning, and had had to rest three times. He felt quite himself again, but consented to having an attendant in his bedroom after the next day. That evening he conducted the usual prayer meeting in No. 3, and afterwards went to bed. Fifty-six years afterwards, in the *Report* for 1954, part of a letter from a former worker is quoted: 'I had the privilege of living in the same house as Mr. Müller, (No. 3, South Wing) and I think I must have been one of the last to see him alive. I was a pupil teacher at the time, and on the Wednesday evening was running up the stairs, singing 'I know not what awaits me, God kindly veils my eyes,' when on nearing the top of the first flight, I was conscious of a dark figure standing quite still. It was Mr. Müller on the way from the prayer meeting to his bedroom. He waited until I reached him, and then, shaking hands with me, said "I am so glad to see you so happy, but you must not run up the stairs two at a time, you may hurt yourself." The next morning, when the maid went to his room, it was found that the Lord had taken him home.'

He was found dead on the floor by the side of his bed. He had evidently got out of bed for a glass of milk and a biscuit which were always placed on his dressing-table at night, and had been seized with a fainting attack from which he had never recovered. The table cloth was disarranged and articles were scattered on the floor, suggesting that he had clutched at the cloth as he fell. The doctor put the time of his death at between five and six o'clock in the morning.

The news of his death, coming so unexpectedly, created a sensation throughout Bristol, and was the general topic of conversation for days. On the following Sunday, allusion of some kind was made to him in practically every pulpit, Anglican and Free Church, in the city and in many churches the Dead March was played.

His funeral, which took place on Monday, March 14th, surpassed anything that had been seen in Bristol before. Not that the funeral itself was a grand one; nothing could have been more simple, and there were no flowers by his own request. But the popular tribute to him was

154

impressive beyond description. Shutters were up in all the main streets. Flags were at half-mast on Bristol Cathedral and other churches. Muffled peals were rung. Tens of thousands of people lined the route along which the funeral procession was to pass.

Perhaps the most impressive tribute to him was the manifest grief of the orphans. In the funeral sermon, his son-in-law referred to 'those dear fatherless and motherless children who, when I faced them this morning at nine o'clock, so filled the air with their sobs that I scarcely knew when I should begin.' And when hundreds of the older orphans walked in the funeral procession, so many of them were observed to be still in tears that even strong men were affected by the sight.

The first part of the funeral service was at Bethesda, and the latter part at Arno's Vale Cemetery, where George Müller was buried in an ordinary grave, by the side of his two wives. The headstone afterwards put up was paid for by past and present orphans, and was a simple one in accordance with his own wish. Mr. Wright had to check the flow of subscriptions, which soon more than covered the cost.

There were numerous references in the Press, some of which are quoted at the end of the *Autobiography*, and include notices from the *Times* and *Daily Telegraph*. One worth quoting in part is that of the *Western Daily Press*

'Never was a philanthropist with less of fanaticism and more of method. His bearing and speech were not those of an emotional enthusiast who would incur heavy liabilities with a light heart; indeed, had he been such a man, his life would have been less surprising than it was; it was his calmness and confidence, associated with the most careful watchfulness over expenditure and most businesslike habits, that presented a combination of qualities altogether unique and wholly surprising. The sound of Mr. Müller's work has gone out into all lands, and it is simply impossible to try to estimate the extent of his influence, directly or indirectly, which he exerted in the course of his long life.' This tribute does justice to his character on the natural plane, and to that extent describes him very well. It virtually passes over his spiritual gifts, but so do the other papers, which all regard him as pre-eminently a philanthropist. The only exception is the *Liverpool Mercury*. 'Upon Ashley Down can be seen a substantial block of buildings where thousands of orphan children have been fed, clothed and educated out of funds which have poured in without any influential committee or organization, without appeal or advertisement of any sort, except, perhaps, the published story of the founder's life. How was this wonder accomplished? Mr. Müller has told the world that it was the result of 'Prayer'. The rationalism of the day will sneer at this declaration; but the facts remain, and remain to be explained. It would be unscientific to belittle historical occurrences when they are difficult to explain, and much juggling would be needed to make the Orphanages on Ashley Down vanish from view.'

Most of the *Daily Telegraph*'s summing-up of Müller's life was accurate and good, apart from its opening sentence which describes him as 'a remarkable, if comparatively unknown man, who has ended his labours and laid down the cares of an anxious though cheerful life at the great age of ninety-three.' If any obituary notice could have made George Müller turn in his grave, that would. He never ceased repudiating the notion that he was burdened, or full of cares, or anxious. He had cast his cares on the Lord, and habitually lived with peace in his soul without anxiety. The trouble was that people simply could not believe it. They could not take him at his word. In his place they would have been chronically anxious themselves, and so, naturally, he *must* be anxious, whatever he might choose to say!

CHAPTER TWELVE

THE MAN AND HIS INFLUENCE

As will have become evident to the reader by now George Müller was essentially a 'Bible Christian'. All his religious exercises were based on the Bible. Prayer began with Bible-reading; a slow and careful study of some passage verse by verse, which passed into meditation, which in turn passed into petition and thanksgiving. He was kept from the limitations of the 'proof-text' outlook by his habit of reading steadily through the Bible, taking every day a portion of the Old Testament and a portion of the New Testament, and always continuing from where he had left off. He was convinced that this was the only way in which to gain a balanced view of the whole. When he was ninety-one he recorded that he had read through the Bible considerably more than a hundred times. Incidentally, he must have had marvellous eyesight. In the Museum at Müller House is one of his Bibles, with print so tiny as to be practically invisible. His wife used one exactly like it, so probably these Bibles were in use during their earlier married life, while they were still young. Nevertheless, few people of any age nowadays could read such print.

George Müller's method of discovering God's will on any point was, first of all to bring himself to a state in which he had no will of his own in the matter. Next, he would seek the guidance of the Holy Spirit by means of Bible study. 'If the Holy Ghost guides us at all,' he said, 'He will do it according to the Scriptures and never contrary to them.' Then he would take circumstances into account, as these often plainly indicated God's will. Throughout, he would pray that God would reveal His will. All this would eventually bring him to a deliberate decision, and frequently an accompanying sense of peace was in itself a guarantee that the decision was the right one. He would feel then absolutely certain that he was meant to proceed with the plan, whatever it might be, and if money were needed to carry it out he would be undisturbed by any delay in its arrival, confident that it would come in God's own time. His faith was always justified by events.

Guidance came not to him only, but to others in relationship to him. Mrs. Rendle-Short, widow of the late Professor A. Rendle-Short who wrote *The Diary of George Müller*, told me the following story. Her two grandfathers were both lifelong friends of George Müller, and one of them, Mr. James Case, lived opposite him in Paul Street, Bristol. Early one morning the two men emerged from their respective houses at the same moment, and Müller crossed over and said to his friend: 'Which way are you going, dear brother, for I will walk with you.' Mr. Case indicated the road he was to take, and they set off. As they turned the corner, a stranger accosted Müller, saying to him, 'George Müller, I think?' Müller bowed and said, 'Yes.' Case naturally withdrew and continued his way alone.

When Müller next met his friend, several days afterwards, he asked him if he recalled the man who had interrupted their walk together. Then he related how the stranger had given him a cheque for a very large sum of money. Mrs. Rendle-Short does not remember the exact sum, but it was something running into four figures. The donor explained that all through the preceding night he had had George Müller on his mind, and had felt half convinced that he should give him a cheque for that particular amount. It seemed to him that God was guiding him to write the cheque, to carry it with him when he went out, and if he met Mr. Müller that morning to take it as a sign that he was to give it to him.

But to Müller also this encounter was a sign from God. He had for some time been seeking to know God's will as to whether he should build another Orphan House, and this large gift of money, so plainly coming through God's guidance of this man whom he had never seen before, brought him the assurance that he was to go forward with his building plans. It was the fact that he had not taken his usual road to Ashley Down that morning, but had been going by a route on which no one could have reasonably expected to meet him, that added the final and most convincing touch.

This is just one more of those instances which taken in isolation might be regarded as a coincidence, but being one of innumerable similar happenings provides impressive evidence of Müller's guided life.

When preparing his sermons, unless some subject or text came especially vividly to his mind, he would pray that he might be guided to one. If this did not soon become apparent, he would then go on with his regular Bible-reading, praying, as he read, for the needed text. He wrote, 'I have even had to go to the place of meeting without a text, and obtained it only a few minutes before I was going to speak; but I have never lacked the Lord's assistance at the time of preaching, provided I had earnestly sought it in private.' Further on he added, 'This I most firmly believe, that no one ought to expect to see much good resulting from his labours if he is not much given to prayer and meditation.' Relevant to this is the following entry under the date of September 28th, 1837, many years before he wrote down his experiences in sermon-preparation. 'I have for a long time been too much outwardly engaged. Yesterday morning I spent about three hours in the vestry of Gideon, to be able to have more time for retirement. I meant to do the same in the afternoon, but before I could leave the house I was called on, and thus one person after another came, till I had to go out. Thus it has been again today.' It is consoling to find that this type of frustration is not peculiar to modern life, and that even George Müller found it exasperating.

In another place in his journal he writes: 'These last few days I have had very little real communion with God, and have therefore been very weak spiritually, and have several times felt irritability of temper. May God in mercy help me to have more secret prayer.'

His health troubles seem to have affected his whole personality at times during those early days in Bristol, as shown by this entry: 'This is the eighth Lord's day since I have been kept from ministering in the word, nor did I think it well, on account of my head, to go to any of the meetings today. Whether I am really getting better I know not, yet I hope I am. My head is yet much affected, though my liver seems somewhat more active. This morning I greatly dishonoured the Lord by irritability, manifested towards my dear wife, and that almost immediately after I had been on my knees before God, praising Him for having given me such a wife.'

Unlike C. H. Spurgeon, his friend and contemporary, Müller was no orator. It was his great spiritual power that carried his message to the hearts of his hearers. Spurgeon himself, referring to one of Müller's addresses, said, 'There was nothing particular in it. The diction and structure of the discourse were not above the average Sunday school teacher, but *there was the man behind it.*'

The following story concerning the two great men of prayer is re-told in the *Report* for 1942.

'C. H. Spurgeon once came to Bristol. He was to preach in the three largest Baptist chapels in the city; and he hoped to collect £300 immediately for his orphanage. He got the money. Retired to bed on the last night of his visit, Spurgeon heard a voice which to him was the voice of the Lord saying, "Give that £300 to George Müller." "But, Lord," answered Spurgeon, "I need it for my dear children in London." Again came the word, "Give that £300 to George Müller." It was only when he said, "Yes, Lord, I will," that sleep came to him. The following morning he made his way to Müller's Orphanage and found George Müller on his knees before an open Bible, praying. The famous preacher placed his hand on his friend's shoulders, and said, "George, God has told me to give you this £300." "Oh!" said Müller, "dear Spurgeon, I have been asking the Lord for that very sum." And those two prayerful men of God rejoiced together. Spurgeon returned to London. On his desk a letter awaited him: he opened it: it contained 300 guineas! "There," he said with joy, "the Lord has returned my £300 with 300 shillings interest."'

Patience and perseverance were as much a part of George Müller's character as was faith. 'It's dogged as does it' might have been his motto, except that he would never have adopted one so non-scriptural. Once convinced that the object of his prayer was according to the will of God, he would pray every day for that prayer to be granted, though the answer might be delayed for years. In one of his addresses, on the text 'Ask, and it shall be given you,' he related some of his personal experiences in prayer. Often, he said, before he left his bedroom, he would receive an answer to some prayer that he had offered that morning. He estimated that at least thirty thousand of his prayers had been answered on the very day, even in the very hour, in which they were made. In other instances he had prayed daily for twenty or thirty years before his request was granted. He said, 'In November, 1844, I began to pray for the conversion of five individuals. I prayed every day without one single intermission, whether sick or in health, on the land or on the sea, and whatever the pressure of my engagements might be. Eighteen months elapsed before the first of the five was converted. I thanked God, and prayed on for the others. Five years elapsed, and the second was converted. I thanked God, and prayed on for the other three. Day by day I prayed for them, and six more years passed before the third was converted. I thanked God for the three, and went on praying for the other two. The man to whom God in the riches of His grace has given tens of thousands of answers to prayer, in the self-same hour or day on which they were made, has been praying day by day for nearly thirty-six years for the conversion of these two individuals, and yet they remain unconverted; for next November it will be thirty-six years since I began to pray for their conversion. But I hope in God, I pray on, and look yet for the answer.' On the page of the *Autobiography* where these words were printed someone added a footnote, as follows 'One of these persons was converted before Mr. Müller's death, and the other only gave clear evidence of conversion after Mr. Müller had passed away.' Only the year before he died, Müller mentioned to Dr. Pierson, afterwards his biographer, that he had been praying for two people every day for over sixty years, who had not to his knowledge yet turned to God. Then he added, 'I have not a doubt that I shall meet them both in Heaven; for my Heavenly Father would not lay on my heart a burden of prayer for them for over three-score years, if He had not concerning them purposes of mercy.'

So important to him was perseverance in prayer that throughout his *Narrative* he records instances of this in other people, whenever such came to his notice. The following entry is typical. August 29th, 1838. 'Among those who were baptized was an aged brother of above 84 years, and one above 70. For the latter his believing wife had prayed 38 years, and at last the Lord answered her prayers in his conversion.'

Pierson touches upon a significant aspect of Müller's temperament. This is how he describes it in his biography, *George Müller of Bristol*, recently re-published by Pickering and Inglis.

'George Müller felt the immense importance of exact statement. Hence he disciplined himself to accuracy. Conscience presided over his *Narrative* and demanded that everything else should be scrupulously sacrificed to veracity. But more than this, God made him, in a sense, *a man without imagination*—comparatively free from the temptations of an enthusiastic temperament. He was a mathematician rather than a poet, an artisan rather than an artist, and he did not see things invested with a false halo. He was deliberate, not impulsive; calm and not excitable. He naturally weighed every word before he spoke, and scrutinised every statement before he gave it form with pen or tongue. And therefore the very qualities that, to some people, may make his narrative bare of charm, and even repulsively prosaic, add to its value as a plain, conscientious, unimaginative, unvarnished and trustworthy statement of facts. Had a man of more poetic mind written that journal, the reader would have found himself constantly and unconsciously making allowances for the writer's own enthusiasm, discounting the facts, because of imaginative colouring. The narrative might have been more readable, but it would not have been so reliable; and in this story of the Lord's dealings, nothing was so indispensable as the exact truth. It would be comparatively worthless, were it not undeniable. The Lord fitted the man who lived that life of faith and prayer, and wrote that life-story, to inspire confidence, so that even sceptics and doubters felt that they were reading, not a novel or a poem, but a history.'

Müller was essentially practical. For instance, in offering counsel on the choosing of a life-partner, after a valuable description of the considerations which should weigh with a Christian, he finishes by saying, 'True godliness without a shadow of doubt, should be the first and absolutely needful qualification to a Christian, with regard to a companion for life. In addition to this, however, it ought to be at the same time calmly and patiently weighed whether, in other respects, there is a suitableness. For instance, for an educated man to choose an entirely uneducated woman, is unwise; for however much on his part love might be willing to cover the defect, it will work out very unhappily with regard to the children.'

He was also intensely alert and observant. Cheats and frauds did not get past George Müller. On one occasion he was one of several people seeing off a party of German friends who were going overseas. He noticed how the cabman, while storing away the small luggage in the hackney cab, thrust several carpet-bags into the hind boot. When the quay was reached, the driver took advantage of the general turmoil to pretend that he had passed over all the luggage to the porter. He had reckoned without Mr. Müller, who had not omitted at the start of the journey to count the packages, which numbered seventeen. The cabman's attention was firmly directed to the boot, and he was obliged, with much confusion, to yield up the bags hidden there, with which he had been hoping to make his escape.

There are few people still living who have a clear enough recollection of Müller, after sixty years, to describe his appearance in any detail. For a reliable pen portrait, it is better to quote the words of Dr. Pierson, who knew him well. The following description is from *George Müller of Bristol*. 'His form was tall and slim, always neatly attired and very erect, and his step firm

168

and strong. His countenance, in repose, might have been thought stern, but for the smile which so habitually lit up his eyes and played over his features that it left its impress upon the lines of his face. His manner was one of simple courtesy and unstudied dignity; no one would in his presence have felt like vain trifling, and there was about him an indescribable air of authority and majesty that reminded one of a born prince; and yet there was mingled with all this a simplicity so childlike that even children themselves felt at home with him. In his speech, he never quite lost that peculiar foreign quality, known as accent, and he always spoke with slow and measured articulation, as though a double watch were set at the door of his lips... Those who saw but little of him, and saw him only in his serious moods, might have thought him lacking in that peculiarly human quality, humour. But neither was he an ascetic nor devoid of that element of innocent appreciation of the ludicrous and that keen enjoyment of a good story which seems essential to a complete man. His habit was sobriety, but he relished a joke that was free of all taint of uncleanness and that had about it no sting for others.'

Here is another contemporary word picture of him, quoted from a pamphlet by Charles R. Parsons, called *Unfailing Triumph*. In this case the speaker was a farmer. 'I was going up

Ashley Hill the other morning when I met Mr. Müller walking towards the city. Had I not known him, I should have said that he was a gentleman of leisure and without a care, so quietly did he walk and so peaceful and stately was his demeanour. The twenty-third Psalm seemed written on his face.' Had he died in middle age, our only guide to his personal appearance might have been verbal descriptions such as these. For most of his life he resisted all the endeavours of his friends and well-wishers far and near, to get hold of his portrait for publication. His reply to such was, 'As I do not wish to direct attention to myself, but to my Lord and Master, I must decline to comply with your request.' When he was about sixty he was offered £500 if he would give such permission, but he refused this offer as he had all the others of the same kind. What finally changed his mind, when he was nearly eighty, must be given in his own words, which, with so many of them italicized, make amusing reading. The paragraph forms part of an introduction which he wrote to his wife's book *The Preaching Tours and Missionary Labours of George Müller*, and the first photograph of him ever published formed the frontispiece to the book.

'In consequence of my steadfast refusal to be photographed, several *representations* of me (for *likenesses* they cannot be called, as I never sat for one of them) have been published, without my knowledge and against my will. A religious periodical, extensively circulated in America, containing one of these portraits, has gone all through the United States. An enterprising photographer tried once to secure my likeness, too, by an instantaneous process, as I was driving in an open carriage up a hill, but was foiled in the attempt. A portrait of George Müller also, with a *most doleful* expression of countenance (conveying not the slightest idea of the happy man he really is) has been going the round, and occasionally come before me, even in the houses of my best friends. In the fear of God, therefore, I have come to this conclusion: since the public *insist* upon having a portrait of me, whether I like to give it or whether I do not, let my beloved Christian friends at least have a photograph that is a *real* and not a false representation of their unworthy brother in Christ! and, especially, let it be one with a pleasant, cheerful expression of countenance, that will glorify and not dishonour the Lord I love; for our very *faces* even should show forth His praise.'

His love for children, and his sympathy for them, reveals itself in chance sentences. Here is one entry. 'At the end of the year 1865 the whooping-cough appeared among the 450 girls of the New Orphan House No. 3... Parents and others, who have an affectionate heart, and who feel for the suffering of children, can easily suppose how our hearts were affected, when we heard these dear children labouring under this trying malady. But while we thought it right to take all necessary precautions with regard to the spread of the disease, and to use the needed remedies; yet our chief and universal remedy was again resorted to. We trusted in God, and betook ourselves to Him, and we were not confounded. When it is considered that we had 1,150 orphans in the three houses, and that the whooping-cough was so general in Bristol and the neighbourhood, and in many instances so fatal, the hand of God, in answer to constant daily prayer for many months regarding this disease is marked enough, in that we had only in all the three houses seventeen cases of whooping-cough, and that only one child died in consequence of the whooping-cough, this dear little girl having constitutionally very weak lungs and a tendency to consumption, which followed whooping-cough.'

Another entry in the *Narrative* shows an understanding of the needs of children that was a great deal less common in 1846 than it is today. Müller is here enumerating the reasons for moving from Wilson Street. 'We have no proper playgrounds in Wilson Street. There is one playground, which, however, is only large enough for the children of one house at a time; but as there are children in four houses who ought to have the benefit of it, we cannot arrange so that all the children have the full benefit of that playground, as the meals, the school hours, the weather and other hindrances interfere. The dear orphans ought, I know, to be trained in habits of industry, but children are children, and need to be treated as such; and they should, on account of their health, have the full benefit of a playground. But this they cannot have in Wilson Street; and to take them out into the fields for the benefit of bodily exercise, as we have been in the habit of doing, is often very inconvenient.'

A letter received by George Müller on March 19th, 1870, soon after the death of his first wife, shows how the orphans regarded them. 'Received from one of the first orphans under our care, who has been a believer in the Lord Jesus for about 28 years, 5s. for Missions, 1Os. for the orphans, and 5s. for myself, with the following letter: "Dear Mr. Müller, Not from ingratitude is it, I have not written before, but because I knew you had so many letters; but not a particle do I love dear Mrs. Müller less, than those who have written. I think I loved her with you as my parents. True, I never knew my parents, to know what it was to love them; but I do know what it is to love you and her, and to mourn her loss. I know you miss her daily. I miss her going by the house; for I always watched you go by; but now you are alone. I trust it may please God to spare you, for years to come, to us all, as well as your own dear child and family; for oh! it would be a blank indeed, were you removed from us. I remain, yours very respectfully, ..." Another orphan, an old boy, wrote: "Dear Sir, I well remember that, whenever I met Mrs. Müller, when in the Home, it was always a kind word, or pat on the head, etc.; *little* things, some say, but still, such as men remember, that, when boys in a Charity School, it was to give the *home* feeling. My brother wrote to me this week. In his letter is the following: "I read in the *Christian World* of Mrs. Müller's death. It must be a great loss to Mr. Müller. I remember the last time I saw her, when I was leaving the School. She gave me some tracts, talked to me and kissed me;" and I have no doubt all the orphans could give similar little items; enough to fill a book.'

George Müller was often commiserated with over his supposed financial burdens, but he found these among the easiest to bear of all his trials. Other problems which caused him far greater anxiety than the financial ones were: the finding of suitable staff for the Orphanage; difficulties concerning individual children, some of whom were very delicate, and some morally unstable; delay in finding suitable situations for the girls and apprenticeships for the boys; alarming epidemics, such as scarlet fever, and once or twice even smallpox, in the Orphan Houses.

He was involved in complicated problems of other kinds also. One distressing affair was a long-lasting dispute of which he himself left no record. However, Neatby's *History of the Plymouth Brethren* filled in some of the facts, and the rest was related to me by someone acquainted with the whole story.

In the shallow society of the period of the Regency and of the reigns of George IV and William IV there were men and women who revolted against the formal religion of the day, and among these were the people who founded the Plymouth Brethren, to give the movement the name most recognizable to those who do not belong to it. Many of the early leaders of the movement were men of birth and breeding, and several, too, were intellectually brilliant. In spite of this, or possibly because of it, for in that day and age men of rank could seldom brook contradiction, some of them were self-opinionated and stubborn to a degree. The bitterness of their wrangling over points of doctrine, and the harshness of their judgement of those who did not hold the same opinions, makes almost unbelievable reading in this more tolerant age. One such leader of the Brethren was J. N. Darby, an Irishman who had taken high honours at Dublin University. He had studied for the Bar where he had had excellent prospects, but his conscience would not allow him to take a brief lest he should be selling his talents to defeat justice. His intellectual powers were of the highest order. He made a translation of the Bible so scholarly that it was considerably used by those who made the Revised Version.

In Ireland he had been associated with Lady Powerscourt, Sir Edward Denny, J. G. Bellett and C. H. Mackintosh; later, in Plymouth, with B. W. Newton, H. W. Soltau and Dr. Tregellis; all names well-known in the Brethren Movement. Darby had the highest of principles, and was undoubtedly sincere, but he was violently fanatical, and only the Vicar of Bray could have avoided falling out with him. He it was with whom George Müller had a long-drawn-out and wearisome battle. The dispute arose, as have so many religious issues, through the writing of a tract. This particular one was the work of Benjamin Wills Newton, one of the Plymouth Assembly. It was not that Müller approved of the tract and Darby did not. Both of them thought that it contained serious error. But Darby's way of marking his disapprobation was to demand the excommunication not only of Newton, but of the entire Plymouth Assembly for having cherished such a viper in its bosom. Müller, who was not a fanatic like Darby, and who was altogether kinder and more sensible, would not take such an absurd and uncharitable course.

George Müller and Henry Craik, and the

Bethesda Church right up to the present day, adopted the basis of a local church having complete right of self-government instead of being part of a system. Darby strove to fuse all the Brethren churches into a system. It is unnecessary to go into this matter in detail, though it occupied Müller's time and energy through many years. His stand against Darby saved the whole Brethren Movement from passing into dissolution, as indeed Darby's brand of exclusiveness did pass. George Müller, Anthony Norris Groves and Henry Craik were virtually the founders of the Open Brethren movement.

Müller appears to have been markedly unsectarian in his general outlook, and wherever he travelled would preach in any church or chapel where the teaching was based on the Bible. But he laid great stress on the difference between the believer and the unbeliever. To him the believer was one who had accepted our Saviour Jesus Christ, with all that this implies; he, or she, had been born again. Only when this had taken place, he was convinced, could the soul be right with God.

He had started his career as a Lutheran pastor. In Bristol, together with Henry Craik, he had built up at Bethesda one of the earliest assemblies of what are now known as Christian Brethren or Open Brethren. Yet he was at heart a large-minded person. He would preach in any church where he was not expected to do or say anything against his conscience. The Orphan Houses, he never ceased to affirm, were not the Orphan Houses of any particular denomination, but God's. While at Ashley Down the orphans, when they went out to chapel, went to Bethesda; but when they left, they were not instructed to attend none but Brethren meetings, but to go to the nearest church, whether Free Church or Anglican, where the Christian faith as they had learnt it was taught. In 1889 he wrote:

'Further, I aim at the removal of sectarianism, at promoting brotherly love amongst true Christians; and with this object in view go among all real believers, by whatever name they are called, provided they are sound in the foundation truths of our holy faith. Though not agreeing at all with some of their opinions and practices, I nevertheless preach amongst them all, having seen for years how greatly the heart of the Lord Jesus must be grieved by the disunion that exists among his own true disciples. On this account, therefore, I have sought to unite all real believers; but as this cannot be done by standing aloof from our brethren in Christ, until they see eye to eye with us on every point, I have gone amongst them, and have united with them, in so far as nothing has been required of me which I could not do with a good conscience.'

What impact did George Müller make upon the other great evangelists and philanthropists of his day? He was so self-effacing, so careful to avoid advertisement of himself or his work, that he was probably not so well-known as those who accomplished far less. In certain circles his name was known all over the world, but it did not become a household word as did Barnardo's. Dr. Barnardo himself had a deep respect for George Müller, and visited him in Bristol more than once, to draw upon Müller's long experience when Barnardo was establishing his own orphanages.

Nevertheless, many prominent people, as for example Lord Derby, Lord Salisbury and Lord Hampton, visited and admired the Homes on Ashley Down. Charles Dickens, too, once went there. He had heard a rumour of the sort that circulates wherever charitable institutions are concerned; in this case to the effect that the orphans were starved. With his usual thoroughness Dickens set himself to investigate the matter in person. Müller received him with courtesy, and as soon as he understood the purport of Dickens' inquiries, decided to let demonstration rather than argument prove the falsity of the report. He sent for a subordinate, handed him a bunch of keys, and requested that Mr. Dickens might be shown over any of the five Orphan Houses he chose to see. This was done, and Dickens went away entirely reassured.

The last point to be touched upon is the far-reaching influence of George Müller's life and work. His influence has been incalculable.

In 1857 a copy of the *Narrative* fell into the hands of a young Irishman, James McQuilkin, who had found Christ only about a year previously. McQuilkin was profoundly impressed by Müller's experiences of the power of prayer, and himself started to pray for a spiritual companion. Another man of similar outlook and equal fervour soon joined him. The two young men were speedily joined by others, and they all met regularly for prayer at Kells in County Antrim. From these small beginnings sprang the Evangelical Revival of 1859, which spread all over the British Isles. Thus George Müller might in a sense be said to have started that revival.

Then there was Hudson Taylor, who was much troubled when he became aware, during his first visit to China, of the inadequacy of missionary activity in that vast country. On his return to England on furlough he sought out George Müller for advice and spiritual comfort. It was at this period that he founded the China Inland Mission, which was run on a basis of faith and prayer in the same manner as Müller's own projects. Müller gave Hudson Taylor the encouragement he so much needed, and thereafter supported the missionaries who went out under the auspices of C.I.M. At one time he was supporting thirty-two missionaries.

In 1893 Müller received the following letter: 'Dear Mr. Müller, Having had the pleasure of meeting you in Japan, in which country I have been living for the last seven years, I should like to see you again, and tell you something of the Orphanage which Mr. Ishii is now carrying on in Okayama, which is really one of the results of your visit, and of the account you gave, while you were in Tokio, of the wonderful way God has provided for your orphans in Bristol.' Müller adds, 'Mr. Ishii, a Christian Japanese, acts now on the same principles on which I labour myself in the orphan work; he has about 150 children under his care, and waits daily upon God for their support.'

In the *Report* for 1922 is described how a woman in Finland was running a small orphanage on a basis of faith and prayer. In her case it was reading a biography of George Müller which had given her the inspiration to start the Home.

One more example, from an entry in the *Report* for 1954, reveals how George Müller's influence is felt even down to our own day. 'We are delighted to receive today a gift of £1 from a former worker in our Nursery who is now a member of the staff of an Orphanage in Australia. The fact which delights us so much is that the Children's Home with which she is connected was begun many years ago by a former worker in these Homes (Miss F. M. Dalwood). It was started, and continues today, on exactly the same basis of faith in God as the work started by our founder. And still more interesting is the fact that the Superintendent is an old No. 1 boy.'

George Müller, surviving as he did to the age of ninety-two, had the reward of being allowed to see the fruit of his labours to an extent granted to few people. On his tours he frequently met with those who had once been under his care; men now doing well in their trade or profession, and women who were valued domestic servants, if they were not already happily married; most of them steadfast Christians. In numerous cases an old boy had married an old girl, so strong was the tie which bound together those who had had the common background of Ashley Down. Many former orphans sent each year the money to support one of the present ones. This was £12 per annum in the early days, but rather more in later years. Letters of appreciation from employers of both old boys and old girls were often received.

In San Francisco Müller met again with a young man, Wilkinson by name, who had been brought up in the Orphan Houses, and who, he was informed, had worked and witnessed in a remarkably fearless manner in the difficult environment of an American naval gunboat. In the same paragraph he tells how, on preaching tours in England, Scotland and Ireland, he had met converted orphans in every one of the large cities in which he had preached, and that sometimes ten or fifteen at one time would come up to shake hands with him. But perhaps the most moving re-encounter is noted down on October 19th, 1893. 'I saw yesterday the first orphan I received, fifty-seven years and seven months since. She is now a widow, and seventy-one years of age.'

Müller made his last Will just three years before he died. It begins thus:

'I, George Müller, Minister of the Gospel and Founder and Director of the Five New Orphan Houses on Ashley Down, Bristol, England, erected and fitted up for the accommodation of 2,050 orphan boys and girls bereaved of both parents by death, and for 112 assistants and servants, declare that this document is my last Will (setting aside all former Wills) which I am now writing.'

Then follow detailed instructions, in which he directs that the work shall be carried on on the same principles on which he founded it. He appoints James Wright to succeed him as sole Director, to be his executor and to be the sole legatee of his personal estate. This was, at his death, only about £60 in money, and books and furniture worth £100.

The Will ends with these impressive sentences. 'I have finished this my last Will and Testament with my own hand, and now in finishing it I cannot help admiring God's wondrous grace in bringing me to the knowledge of the Lord Jesus when I was an entirely careless and thoughtless young man twenty years and five weeks old, and that He has kept me in His fear and truth for sixty-nine years and four months, allowing me the great honour for so long a time of serving Him. And now in the prospect of eternity I confess that my only hope of salvation is faith in the merits and in the atoning death of my precious adorable Lord Jesus Christ. I sign this my last Will before two witnesses, both of whom are present at the same time. Ashley Down, Bristol, March 16th, One thousand, eight hundred and ninety-five (1895).

George Müller'

CHAPTER THIRTEEN

LIFE IN THE ORPHAN HOUSES

This chapter begins with an eye-witness account of the work on Ashley Down in the early days. The following extracts are from what is probably the sole surviving copy of a twopenny pamphlet, entitled, 'A Visit to the New Orphan House, Ashley Down, Bristol', published in 1856, only seven years after No. 1 was opened.

'On Sabbath mornings, between 10 and 11, may be seen long files of children, both male and female, slowly wending their way along Maudlin-lane and Park-row, to the chapel in Great George Street, under the pastoral care of the Revs. Henry Craik and George Müller. The boys and girls are very neatly and becomingly dressed, with nothing to distinguish them from others in their general appearance, except that the fact of between 200 and 300 children being clothed alike, evidences that they are under one common superintendence...' 'On Wednesday afternoons the Institution is thrown open, and parties are in attendance to guide strangers through every department of the building... The decent mechanic and the millionaire are equally welcome, and treated with equal courtesy. Let us give the results of one of these Wednesday afternoon visits. We met at the door, a little after two o'clock, a pretty numerous party of all ranks in life, waiting for admission. When the doors were opened, we found ourselves in a very small hall, from whence a stone staircase leads up into a spacious room in the central buildings, where the visitors wait for their guide. This room is a perfect square, with the four angles taken off by the width of the windows, which we found looked into large pitched play-courts, with covered sheds for the children's use in wet weather. One court we saw was appropriated to infants of both sexes, a number of whom were toddling about under the charge of two or three older girls; another to girls; the third to boys; while the fourth window overlooks that part of the garden through which the visitors approach.

'Our guide entered, and took charge of the forty or fifty who had by this time assembled. Those who arrived after this time would wait for another cicerone; and when needed, three parties, at intervals of half an hour, are taken round in one day.

'We proceeded into the Infants' Day Room, where we found a tribe of little things, under the care of a nurse. Ranged round one side of this room are a number of little basket beds, for the use of the youngsters when tired of play.

'We found in one room about half a dozen boys, under the care of a female, quietly and busily engaged in the very necessary employment of darning stockings, which attracted the sympathy of the female part of the company most wonderfully. One lady, advanced in life, was quite carried away by her enthusiasm—"One thread up and one thread down, is the very perfection of darning." Some, perhaps, of these boys may at a future time be in the navy, others may chance to be emigrants; and we can hardly estimate the value of this

humble but necessary art in such circumstances. Even in the very common experience of
apprentices in this country, it will often prove
of very great advantage to them. In any case we
admire the practical wisdom that insists, even in
mending stockings, on teaching the best way.

'In the younger department are pigeon-holed
cupboards for putting away their toys, when out
of use. They were well-furnished with nearly
every description that a general shop could
supply.

'The washing-places, we observed, are
furnished with baths, and on the walls is hung
each child's little bag, numbered, with comb
and hair-brush. The most scrupulous care is
evidently bestowed to ensure thorough
cleanliness of both persons and linen, as well as
to guard against the communication of any
infectious juvenile complaints from personal
contact.

'In going through this most interesting
establishment we were most forcibly impressed
with the entire absence of a *pauperised* look in
the dress and appearance of the children. The
hair of the girls is kept beautifully neat, such as
we could fancy a *mother's* love had attended to;
and there was a cheerful looking-up at the
visitors, and a heart-smile on the young faces,
which prove indisputably that both in Principal
and Assistants the spring of action is Love, and
that the presiding and pervading spirit which

rules the entire establishment is the Law of Kindness. In fact, it is impossible to help being thoroughly convinced that the best of practical management exists in every department, and that everyone engaged in the work is admirably fitted for his duties, and has a hearty unselfish love of the work for its own sake.'

Now, more than a century after that description was penned, we look back across the intervening years and try to assess what life was like for the inmates of those Orphan Houses. It is only possible to pass judgement on this if the orphanage is considered in its contemporary setting. Any attempt to compare it with present-day homes for needy children is bound to be misleading. It must be seen against its nineteenth-century background in order to gain a true picture.

Looked at in this way it is seen to be, not an old-fashioned institution, but a pioneer among orphanages. When the first Orphan House was opened in Wilson Street, there were scarcely any Orphan Houses in this country. There were homes for foundlings, and there were the workhouses, little happier than prisons. Orphanages as such, so plentiful by the eighteen-eighties, hardly existed in 1836.

We moderns, gazing at those vast buildings, regard them as little better than barracks. But then Cottage Homes had come into fashion before most of us were born. As early as the turn of the present century, it was already being thought undesirable to herd children together in such large numbers. George Müller, however, in the 1850's when the new Orphan Houses began to go up, was offering a modern amenity to the hundreds of parentless children who would otherwise have been either homeless, or grudgingly offered a corner in the overcrowded home of some relative.

It is customary now to regard this housing of children in one huge building as an evil that may be necessary where hundreds are destitute and in need of shelter, but indefensible in any other circumstances. This view is, generally speaking, the justifiable one; nevertheless there is another side to the picture. The children's home of today, in which no effort is spared to give each inmate the fullest possible life, and in which the annual cost per child would have supported twenty orphans of the past, is a post-war development, and is outside the scope of what we are trying to investigate. The older cottage homes were certainly more intimate and, if well-equipped, cosier places than large institutions, but life in them could be deadly dull. Anyone who has been to a well-conducted large boarding school will know that, though lacking in certain home comforts, its atmosphere is stimulating. Provided that the principal and assistant staff are upright, conscientious Christians, with a real concern for the children's welfare, then even the unavoidable regimentation does not prevent there being something vitalizing about the very air of the place. Life is harder than in a small school but it can often be jollier. Then, too, in such a large group, the challenge of religious ideals and the consequent demand for a high moral standard will often win a response from the older pupils to a degree seldom encountered in private life. The exhilaration this produces in the adolescent needs to have been experienced to be believed.

This quotation from a letter from an old orphan girl shows how she, and no doubt many of the children, regarded the buildings which housed them. She is writing at the time when the Scattered Homes have been started, and the Ashley Down houses are soon to close. 'I've been wondering what is going to happen to those lovely large Homes: to me every stone is a prayer... I was in No. 2. I had a most wonderful time there.'

When Müller built the five Houses they were in the midst of fields, almost alone on the breezy heights of Ashley Down. But building was going on in and around Bristol at a rapid pace, and at last the Orphanage stood in a sea of houses, which quite spoilt the outlook for the children. I have seen a letter, written in 1918, by the junior boys to the Director on George Müller's birthday, as was customary, in which one sentence runs: 'We do miss the fields.' Evidently one of the last of the surrounding fields was being built over.

What was the food like in those Orphan Houses? By modern standards, the menu was totally inadequate and most monotonous. But here again comparison must be made, not with the variety to be found in present-day school meals, but with the diet of the children of those far-off days. In private homes, even those of the rich, the schoolroom breakfast was likely to be 'bread and milk' with unvarying regularity, and the only relish would be 'the top of father's egg' as often as your turn came round in a family of five or six children, when you went down to bid your parents good-morning in the breakfast room. The food at fee-paying boarding schools was proverbial for its poor quality, and was likely to be strictly limited in quantity.

At the Orphan Houses the main articles of diet seem to have been bread, with treacle or dripping; oatmeal; potatoes and other vegetables; stew; corned beef; rice. Bread was made then not from processing ingredients, but from genuine stone-ground wheaten flour, and the potatoes and vegetables were grown on naturally fertilized land, giving them a flavour and food value that seems to have vanished from the earth now.

The orphans' only beverage, except on rare occasions, was milk and water, which sounds unattractive, though children do not seem to mind that type of drink. I recall a very good boarding school where the boys' drink at breakfast and tea time never varied. It was, for each boy, about half a cup of milky and watery tea, always poured out and cooling rapidly before the boys sat down to their meal. I never heard one of them object to it.

The orphans' main grumble, if asked, would probably have been the absence of sweet things, but there again the limitation of sugar was in accordance with the notions of that period. 'Too much sweet stuff is not good for children' was a favourite catchword. I think that there is no doubt that there was too little fat and sugar in the diet, and far too little fruit. Nevertheless, the children seem mostly to have thrived, and people used constantly to comment on their healthy appearance and glossy hair.

Several children died every year, but here again it would not be quite fair to compare the Homes with an ordinary school. The most common cause of death of the parents was tuberculosis, and in a great many cases it had carried off both the father and mother. Often a whole family, orphaned in this way would be admitted, sometimes in a very poor state of health, and many new arrivals were already infected by the disease without its yet being apparent. It seems amazing that lay people, quite apart from the medical profession, did not tumble to the fact that tuberculosis is a contagious disease. Right to the end of the century, in private houses, healthy young people were sharing beds with tubercular patients. In the light of such considerations, twelve or fourteen deaths a years in the five Homes does not seem so shocking. Perhaps it speaks of a healthy regime that more did not die. Müller tells us that many of the children were in a very delicate state on being admitted, but that most of them soon gathered strength. He speaks as if the death rate were low compared with other institutions, and gives thanks when there have been 'only twelve deaths this year'. It is just another illustration of the differing times in which we live. Even one death a year in a school of five hundred nowadays would be the cause of much head-shaking.

Particular care was always taken of the sick children in the infirmaries, which were situated on the top floor of each House. As mentioned before, many of the children arrived already infected with tuberculosis, though it had not been as yet detected. Others, though not infected, had no doubt inherited a predisposition to it. These unfortunate little creatures spent long periods, in some cases several years, in the infirmary, and every year some died of the disease, which was by far the chief cause of mortality among orphans. It is pleasant to learn that special attention was given to the more delicate of the children, even those who were well enough to take part in the normal life of the school. They were given such extras as milk and bread and butter at mid-morning, and were excused such exertions as scrubbing floors, or taking the long walk to Bethesda if they were unequal to it. With such care many a sickly child grew into a robust one. Sister Petherick, whose life story is quoted farther on, gradually developed from the most fragile of infants into a strong, healthy girl, ideally fitted to train as a hospital nurse.

In 1855 four young children were admitted in such a deplorable state of malnutrition that it was doubtful whether it would be right to admit them at all, as they seemed cases for a hospital rather than for a school. But it seemed inhuman to send them away, so they were taken in and tenderly cared for. In a few weeks they had improved so much as to be unrecognizable, and as Pierson says 'there were with God's blessing probably four less graves to be dug.'

The clothes provide another interesting debating-point. Where an old-established orphanage with a picturesque uniform is concerned, there is always liable to be a clash of opinion between those who look at the matter from the aesthetic viewpoint, and those who look at the matter from the practical. The old uniform at Müller's was in the style of the usual dress of children in the 1830's. It undoubtedly gave the orphans a grace and a dignity, and as it became antiquated, a sentimental appeal, which the modern dress introduced in 1936, with its knee-length skirts and squashed-on hats, entirely lacked.

The older boys wore a navy blue Eton jacket, with a waistcoat buttoning up to the white starched collar, both of heavy serge; brown corduroy trousers; caps with a glazed peak; and in bad weather, short cloaks. Each boy had three suits.

The small boys, up to about eight or nine years old, wore for everyday a garment which seems a strange choice from the practical point of view. It was a plainly-cut smock, with no collar, in white or unbleached cotton. Possibly, being white it could soon be boiled and restored to its original purity, but who, knowing boys, can help suspecting that it spent much of its time anything but white. Blue serge shorts, socks and strap shoes completed the costume. For best wear, the little boys discarded their smocks, and wore Norfolk suits with broad Eton collars, in which they looked most attractive. Their caps were the same as the older boys.

The girls' outdoor dress in cold weather was a long cloak in green and blue plaid; in mild weather a shepherd's plaid shawl took the place of the cloak; in hot weather, for best wear, the dress was a thin one of dull lilac cotton, over which was worn a small cape or tippet of the same material, a tiny ruff at the neck. Throughout the year the girls wore bonnets of natural-coloured straw. To each bonnet was attached a long strip of thin material with a green and white checked pattern, which formed a band across the top, crossed at the back and was stitched at the sides, so that the two ends formed the strings by which the bonnet was tied on.

The everyday dresses for girls of all ages were of navy cotton covered with small white dots, to which for walking out was added a white tippet when the weather was too warm for cloaks or shawls. Indoors, the girls up to fourteen wore blue-checked gingham pinafores, cut high to the neck and buttoning behind. The girls over fourteen, who had left the schoolroom and were called 'House Girls', wore aprons with strings, to distinguish them from their juniors. The most senior girls, those who were due to leave the Homes for situations within a few months, were known as 'Cap Girls', and wore caps, aprons to the waist and white collars. Every girl had five dresses.

The stockings were all hand-knitted by the girls; black wool for winter, and white cotton for summer. A pair of these white stockings is to be seen in the Museum at Müller House. The shoes were mostly of the ankle-strap style.

With the old uniform the girls had no waterproofs, and in doubtful weather there was one cotton umbrella for every two children. The privilege of carrying the umbrella was not one that was eagerly competed for. The walk on wet days was often a quiet squabble, as the more strong-minded of each pair in the crocodile pressed the umbrella into her partner's unwilling hand.

The girls' hair was managed rather cleverly, considering that hundreds of heads of hair had somehow to be made presentable every day. The tiny girls had theirs almost as short as a boy's, but beautifully glossy and well-brushed. Those from about eight years old up to eleven had a dutch bob, with centre parting and fringe, such as they could comb into place themselves without assistance. The older girls, who were capable of doing their own hair, were allowed to grow it to shoulder length or longer, and hold it back with a velvet ribbon band. The most senior girls put their hair up.

The nursery infants do not seem to have been always in uniform, so probably the many babies' clothes which must have been sent to the Homes were fully utilized. Some photographs show little groups of toddlers decked out with loving care in frilled and embroidered pinafores which have no suggestion of the pauper about them.

In the very early days, while the uniforms

were still in the style of current fashions for children, the orphans were probably well pleased with their clothes. They were warm and practical, and the materials, though coarse, were good. I have handled some of these materials, which were all of types no longer obtainable. Up to the time of George Müller's death, the styles, though somewhat old-fashioned, were not entirely unlike those worn by children in private homes. Flora Thompson, in her book *Lark Rise*, tells how village girls in the eighties still wore dresses to their ankles, and looked askance at a companion clad in one of the short dresses then coming into fashion. Pinafores, in much the same style as those worn by the Müller girls, were still almost universal. It was as the twentieth century moved on its way that the uniform began to make the children remarkable, and caused them to be the cynosure of all eyes wherever they went. Naturally they disliked this. It made them feel odd when they went out into the streets of Bristol for walks or to go to chapel. Who can be surprised at their delighted smiles as they pose for their photograph before starting for a walk dressed in their new uniforms in 1936. The uniform in question is that of the average schoolgirl of the period, surely one of the most unbecoming costumes ever designed for the teenage girl; skirt above the knees, black shoes and stockings, hats like pudding basins with small brims pulled down nearly to the eyes. No wonder those who love the picturesque lamented the abandonment of the old style of dress, but how mistaken they were to do so, nevertheless. Children are not meant to be walking museum-pieces. It was entirely for their happiness and well-being that some resolute person forced through the change, and since then their clothes have always been contemporary in fashion.

The school curriculum consisted of Scripture, reading, writing, arithmetic, English grammar, history, geography, Swedish drill and singing. Sewing and knitting were taught with great care, the latter to the boys as well as to the girls. The boys had to knit themselves three pairs of socks before leaving the Homes, which rule was the cause of many groans from the less industriously-minded. In one photograph, showing the boys in their playground, one luckless youth of about fourteen is seen, needles and sock in hand, knitting in the midst of his scuffling companions. No doubt there is some attractive apprenticeship he hopes to be considered for, if only he can complete his tale of socks. If not, it will be offered to another boy, and he will have to remain on at school, still knitting! Mr. W. Tidball, himself an old Number 4 boy, told me how sock-knitting even came in as a form of barter. On a certain day in the year a large apple dumpling was given to each boy, and those of the type for whom one is never enough would say: 'You give me your dumpling and I'll knit you a pair of socks!'

The following is from the *Report* for 1916:

'From a former orphan, once in the Boys' Department of Wilson Street, seven pairs of socks beautifully knitted by himself. He writes: "Will you kindly accept these for the dear little orphans, as a thank-offering to the Lord for all His marvellous care and kindness to me for so many years, now in my 86th year, and for having opened that beautiful home for me in Wilson Street; and in which Home I was taught to knit."'

Singing was carefully taught throughout the orphanage by a special singing master. Even in 1856 the author of the pamphlet already quoted could write, 'Both boys and girls sang several simple pieces very correctly.' About sixty years ago there was *The Ashley Down Song Book*, a copy of which may be seen in the museum at Müller House. A glance through this shows it to be an innocuous if not very stimulating collection of songs, typical of the average school song book of the period, with tonic-sol-fa notation. It is doubtful if the music sung, either secular or sacred, could be described as of high artistic value, but the quality of the singing was almost certainly good. The orphans were trained to make perfection their aim in all their lessons and other duties, and were therefore almost certainly accustomed to concentrate, and no doubt this applied to singing lessons, too. When three or four hundred young voices were uplifted together, the effect must have been fine, and when fifteen hundred sang in one building, as in Bethesda Chapel at the orphans' united service on Good Friday, it can have been hardly less than magnificent. I once heard about 200 orphans sing a hymn in the great dining-room of Number 3, and there was a radiance in their tone that lingers in the memory.

The orphans were brought up on the Bible, which they read constantly, and studied with teachers who believed in it with all their hearts. Every day each child had to memorize a verse of Scripture, being prepared to recite on Sunday the six verses learnt on the six preceding days. Many, writing in after days, spoke of the love of the Bible acquired at Ashley Down.

In 1907 a boy, apprenticed in Wales, wrote to one of the schoolmasters at the Orphan Houses:

'The Vicar says that the boys from our School are the most scholarly and decently-behaved boys he has seen in all his ministry. He says we have the Bible on our tongues. All this is due to you and the other masters.'

In 1908, from Liverpool, came a donation of two guineas for the orphans, with a letter from an old boy, which included these words:

'Thirty-four years ago I was born again,

through the Word of God, read and commented on by a fellow-orphan in the classroom of No. 4, and today as by the grace of God, I am enabled to look back over those years, I can again testify to the presence and the power of the living God, who has kept me until this hour.'

In 1939, from Walworth, 10s., with this letter: 'It will be sixty-one years on the 23rd of this month since I left the loving godly influence and shelter of No. 4 New Orphan House. Bless God for all that love and care bestowed upon me; for the love I gained of God's Holy Word, and all that it has meant to me through all these years. There is in my heart one desire, if it should be the will of God, to see the dear familiar scenes of my boyhood days once again. May this year be crowned with an abundant harvest of dear girls and boys won for their loving Saviour. Your old and grateful orphan.'

'Every minute of the week I spent in Bristol that I could spare was given to a walk past the Homes, reviving old memories, and sighing with mixed regret and happiness. Regrets to think of the Houses passing to other hands, and yet happiness that I and thousands of others were there, and the love it gave us of the Bible.

'Many, many times have I said "thank you" for the grounding of faith which was all about us, and was lived so wonderfully by directors,

202

matrons, teachers and workers.'

Discipline seems to have been strict, but not harsh. Punishments were fairly frequent, including the cane, but old orphans to whom I have spoken, while they remember the cane's existence, seem to have little recollection of experiencing it themselves, which seems to suggest that it was not employed unduly. There was some bullying and a certain amount of unauthorized fagging even among the girls; nevertheless it is the memory of the crowd of friends and companions, with all the jollity and absence of boredom that this implies, that forms one of the happiest memories of so many, and which was the feature of daily life most missed when the time came to exchange membership of an Orphan House for that of a private household. Many a young person, in the comfortable dullness of a good situation, felt this deprivation for weeks, months and even years after leaving Ashley Down.

Occasionally it was found necessary to expel a really refractory child, and return him or her to relatives, as the Homes were not reformatories, and such children had a corrupting influence on the others. But expulsion was always a last resort, and after a long period spent in attempted reclamation; and even after the offender had left, he was followed by the prayers of those who tried to help him.

Not infrequently the one who had been

expelled voluntarily renewed contact with the Orphan Houses later on. In the 1928 *Report* appears the following:

'From an old orphan, £1: A former orphan boy, who was dismissed forty-seven years ago for continued disobedience. He came last evening to No. 4, to show his wife the place where he was a boy, and especially the schoolroom, where he described his dismissal by Mr. Müller and Mr. Müller's final word, with tears, of "I am sorry! God bless you." He traces all his continued employment ever since to this blessing by Mr. Müller!'

Each of those Orphan Houses was not only run separately from the other, but each contained, in its different wings, two or more separate schools, the children of which gathered together only in the dining-room for meals, and for daily and Sunday services, etc. The arrangement of the children throughout the five Houses varied at times over the years. At the time of George Müller's death they were apportioned as follows:

Number 1 Girls over eight
         Boys over eight   Totalling
         Boys under eight   300 children

Number 2 Girls over eight
         Girls under eight   400 children

Number 3 Girls over eight	450 children

Number 4 Boys over eight	
Boys under eight	
37 House Girls for	450 children
the domestic work	

Number 5 Girls over eight	
Girls under eight	450 children

CHAPTER FOURTEEN

THE ABIDING INFLUENCE OF ASHLEY DOWN

Although the orphans were not told when supplies appeared to be failing, nevertheless they knew that everything they ate, wore and used, came in answer to prayer, and they were well able to believe that God would supply all their need. A former orphan wrote, in 1931, 'What a witness to the loving care of our Heavenly Father. I was in the schools Nos. 2 and 3 eight years. Someone lately asked me if we were ever short of food while there. I said "No". Never one meal was missing, neither did we think there would be, for we knew in whom we trusted.'

The buildings were exceedingly well kept as

regards decoration and repairs, and were spotlessly clean. The children of school age did a certain amount in the way of chores, including floor-scrubbing, but the work of the Institution generally was carried out by the House Girls. These were the girls between fourteen and seventeen who had left the schoolroom to spend their final three years in what was virtually a domestic science school. They did the cooking, laundering, housework, parlour-maid duties and dressmaking. Many of them helped in the nurseries, and a few in the infirmaries. This was their preparation for service later, and few of them left until their seventeenth birthday was past. George Müller had been a man of the world. He knew only too well the defencelessness of an unprotected girl. That was why he kept them in the Home for several years after it would have been possible to have sent them out to service; why he saw to it that they were thoroughly trained for their job, so as to be able to hold their situations when they went to them; and why the Homes generally had about three times as many girls as boys, as he felt that they needed care and protection more.

The House Girls had more privileges than the schoolgirls. Also they were each paid sixpence weekly, though of this, threepence was kept back and banked for them, and on leaving they had the accumulated sum to draw out and take with them to their first post.

The schoolgirls were by turns sometimes given a particular responsibility. There were the 'Clothes Girl', the 'Counterpane Girls', etc. Each 'Clothes Girl' was in charge of the clothes of six children. It was her duty to brush and fold garments before putting them away; to keep the clothes in each locker in apple-pie order, and to put out clean clothes as required. Every washable garment was marked not only with the owner's number, but also with the numbers 'one', 'two', or 'three'. To ensure that every article should be used in rotation, every week was a 'one', 'two', or 'three' week, and the 'Clothes Girls' had to be careful to lay out clothes bearing that week's number. It was methods such as these, which were employed in every department of the Orphan Houses, that kept the Institution running with such economy of money and effort, and at the same time trained the children to be alert, accurate and thorough. The 'Counterpane Girls' carried out comparable duties at stated times each day in the bedrooms.

On leaving, usually between the ages of fourteen and fifteen, each boy was apprenticed to some trade, for which a premium of £13 was paid for him. The masters who took the boys were supposed to be practising Christians, vouched for in this respect in their letters of reference. Those who wrote the references did not always press their inquiries as closely as they should have done, and some boys were not as fortunate in their masters as were others. William Ready, mentioned on another page, was sent to the most saintly of masters, whose influence over him was the making of him morally and spiritually. Mr. W. Tidball, whose story also is told further on, had the ill-fortune to go to a master who proved to be miserly, irreligious and incompetent to teach his trade, which was printing, so that the boy had to pick it up as best he could, almost unaided.

It is easy to say that closer investigation should have been made, but it is hard to see how in practice this could have been carried out, especially in the early days before cars and telephones came into use. Probably two or three hundred situations had to be found every year, and not nearly all could be local. A visit was paid to the prospective employer before the child went, but such cursory inspection does not reveal a true picture of the sincerity or otherwise of religious profession, the food served at the daily meals, or the ability of the master to teach his trade. The boys and girls were encouraged to correspond regularly with those who knew them at the Homes, but even parents find that the absent young person often is not at all communicative about difficulties that might be put right if only his elders knew about them.

Apprenticeships were not sought for by

advertisement, as that might have tended to bring applications from masters who were after the premium rather than the boy. In 1862, Dr. Pierson records, several boys were ready to leave the Homes, but there were no suitable applications for apprentices. Prayer was made, and in due course every one of the eighteen boys was bound over to a Christian master with a regular business, who was ready to receive the boy as one of his family. As the years passed, old orphans who had established themselves began to send to the Homes for apprentices. One who wrote to send a gift of money in 1880 had at that time three orphan boys in his house as apprentices. The girls had no premium paid for them, but they had nearly three years longer in the Homes. They were sent to mistresses who had to give evidence that they were Christian people in the same way as did the boys' masters, and naturally this sometimes worked and sometimes did not. The girl was expected to remain at least one year in her first place. To many a girl, going from the friendly shelter of the Homes into an unfamiliar environment, that year must have been a year of testing.

During the year 1873 a new scheme was launched; that of making converted and otherwise suitable boys into pupil teachers. After five years of preliminary training at the Orphan Houses, during which period they were expected to study hard to improve their general education, they were sent to help at the Scriptural Knowledge Institution's schools at Purton in Gloucestershire. There, while they gained wider experience they worked for their teaching certificates. Next they were brought back to continue at the Orphan Houses, and at last, if they had proved satisfactory throughout their training, they were either appointed as regular masters there, or else put in charge of one of the Day Schools. This plan, which was extended to apply to the girls also, proved a great success, and helped greatly to maintain the supply of Christian masters and mistresses in the Orphan Houses and the Day Schools.

Both boys and girls, on setting out into the world, were provided with a complete outfit; tin trunk, clothes, an umbrella, a Bible, the three volumes of George Müller's *Narrative* (after his death the *Autobiography* was given instead); and half a crown in the case of the boys, the accumulated savings in the case of the girls. Each young person was seen off at the station by a master or matron.

Each department of the five Houses had its own playground. There were also two fields in which the children could play in dry weather. In addition to these fields, there was much land which the boys helped to cultivate.

A swimming bath was opened on June 10th, 1910. It was an anonymous gift, and a truly munificent one, as with its adjoining rooms it cost nearly £5,000. Mr. Bergin, who was then Director, wrote in the *Report* that it was in daily use, to the great benefit and enjoyment of both orphans and teachers. In their letters old orphans often commented thankfully on having been taught to swim while at Müller's. Many of the children gained the Bristol Humane Society's Certificate for Life-Saving.

In many cases whole families, numbering five, six or seven children, were taken into the Homes at one time. What is almost more remarkable is that there were instances of parent and child being brought up there, at an interval of twenty or thirty years. In the 1913 *Report* appears the following letter: (For some years previous to this children had been admitted who had one parent still living: 'I am so grateful for the time my daughter was at Ashley Down. She has now been four years in her first situation since leaving your dear Homes, where my dear late husband was also cared for and brought to a knowledge of the truth as it is in Jesus.' In the 1910 *Report* is a very similar letter concerning a mother and sons all brought up at Ashley Down.

Report (1913). 'The mother of a boy, who has recently left us, writes: "I am anxious to express to all at the Orphanage my gratitude and sincere thanks for all the care and kindness, and the good training my son has received during the eleven years he has been at No. 4; also for the splendid outfit you have so kindly given him, for which I am truly thankful. Also the splendid lot of books, which we shall all love to read. I cannot express in words all the gratitude I feel for all the care and kindness.'''

Living was undoubtedly plain, routine almost unvarying, privacy non-existent, possessions few, freedom restricted, individual attention limited. How then does one account for the following quotations from old orphans' letters, taken at random from *Reports*, and typical of hundreds that have appeared during the past century?

'We were very happy children, and I never cease talking about my old home.'

'Many years ago, to be exact 1875, my father, now 86, became a member of Müller's Orphan Homes. He still cherishes happy recollections of his eight years' stay, and looks back with gratitude to the care, love and instruction he received during those early and impressionable years. He can remember Mr. Müller.'

'Once again memory goes back to Number 5 and the years I spent there; and with thankfulness for the love and care which we had then. The first love of gardening I learnt at Number 5 with my little flower garden.'

'I am so thankful that I have memories of dear Ashley Down, and I hope the present generation will have as good a time as we all had and also that they will grow up to love the dear Home as we all have.'

Not all the children enjoyed it so much, but even those who were irked by the restrictions at the time looked back with gratitude. One man, who was there in the 1930's, told me frankly that he did not like it at the time, but that every year he lives he appreciates more the education and training he received, and he still returns to the Reunions.

There seems little doubt to me that the happiness and contentment enjoyed by so many, and the benefits received by almost all, derived from the atmosphere of love that pervaded the place; love for God and love for man. The members of the staff lived dedicated lives. Prayer and thanksgiving were part of the warp and woof of life there. Again excerpts from the *Report* bear this out. Here is one from a successful business man.

'It is with unbounded gratitude that I continue to thank God for the four to five years I spent in the Homes. The great lessons that we learnt there have been my stay through life; now nearly seventy-two, I cannot put into words the deep gratitude for all that was done for me there, and for having known George Müller in the flesh. I always remember the feeling of great peace when I was in his presence, although I was so young.'

(1939) From London £2. 'for the use of the

dear old home. I've just returned from a fortnight's work in Wiltshire. I did so hope to have time to visit Bristol. Perhaps it is as well as I couldn't get time. I well remember once when Mr. Müller returned from one of his missionary tours the whole lot of us being lined up outside No. 3 to welcome him, and myself a very small child being held up to present to Mrs. Müller a large bunch of honeysuckle. I always follow the scent of honeysuckle, but have never yet found any to come near my memory of that bunch—each and every one looks smaller and much less lovely. Perhaps the dear old home would have looked changed. It was so very beautiful, and my eleven years so very happy. I'd rather keep my memories.'

1922. 'I often look back, twenty years ago now, to the happy fourteen years of my boyhood, passed there in No. 4, and feel I can never repay for those years. I have had much pleasure in revisiting my old Home four times, once during my army leave from France, and I am greatly looking forward to once again visiting the dear old place.'

1928. From Horfield, Bristol, £1. 'With grateful remembrances from an old orphan for the unceasing care received whilst in that dear, happy Home.'

1928. From Nelson, Lancs, £1 with this letter: 'It is with great joy I send you the enclosed, being a regular portion of my

214

pension, just to show you I am very grateful for all dear Mr. Müller did for me in my childhood, and to help in a small way in what you are now doing in his place. God bless you, dear Sir, and my dear old Home. Your very grateful Orphan.'

'I am glad to see a number of orphans remember the dear old Home, in which they spent their happiest days; for truly there have been none happier to me than those spent in the dear Orphan House Number 3. How happy we were in our own little world, brought up in such a holy atmosphere.'

In 1906, a boy apprenticed to a chemist in Nottingham wrote, 'Many thanks for the 'Daily Light' Almanack you so very kindly sent me. I will try to learn the texts in the morning when I get up. I often think of the splendid time I had in the Home. As I look back on my schooldays, just left behind me, I think they were the jolliest days of my life. I have joined a Sunday School class, and go every Sunday.'

1916. From a former orphan: 'I was only a small child then, and am still a child when I think of Ashley Down. It was a lovely, lovely spot ... and no place ever seemed so dear.'

Evidence of the children's happiness and well-being is shown not only by the tributes they themselves afterwards paid, but by those from outside sources as well. *Report* for 1909: 'I want to express my heartfelt gratitude for your kindness to my little protégée, who is so happily settled in No. 2 Orphan House. I have seen her twice since she was received, and have been struck by the change in her little pinched face, and the look of happiness and contentment, which speaks for itself. I trust her mother's prayers will be answered, and the little life yielded to the Saviour.' *Report* for 1912. 'Concerning a girl who left us, the gentleman who applied for her admission writes: "In reading A——'s letter, I cannot help feeling that I ought to repeat my heartfelt thanks to you and those around you for being the means of directing her in the right path. The early possibilities were that she would have been a physical and moral wreck in the slums of Liverpool.' *Report* for 1926: 'From the father of two of our girls, £1 towards their maintenance. After recently visiting them he writes: 'I was delighted, yes, more than delighted, to find them in such good health and spirits, and I must express my heartfelt appreciation of all your obvious care for them in every way.' *Report* for 1905. 'From Christchurch, £2, from a donor who writes: 'Mrs. N. last week took the journey to see her little grand-daughter. She cried with gratitude at seeing the child looking so well and so happy, and in such a lovely home.' *Report* for 1903. 'There came, on the 8th, from Fulham, £2. The donor, a widow, whose two boys had been received into the

Orphan Houses, wrote to Mr. Bergin as follows: "I am writing to thank you for your very kind words to me on June 18th last year, when I was so broken-hearted at parting with my two dear little boys. Now, Sir, I cannot tell you how grateful I am to you, and Mr. Wright, for the beautiful home you have given them. I am so thankful to be able to send you a small gift.'"

This last letter reminds one that as a result of the decision, made in 1901, to admit from that time on not only full orphans, but children bereaved of one parent, the Directors had a painful task to perform which George Müller himself had been spared. They had to receive children from the hand of the surviving parent, and console all parties as best they could. When a widower decided to give up his children, it was generally because he could not cope with them with no wife to help him; where widows were concerned it was more likely to be a case of utter destitution for mother and children because she could not both care for them and go out to earn a living wage. The problem was often complicated by illness, and many of the case histories were heart-rending. Things generally took a decided turn for the better once the children were settled at Ashley Down, and then in many cases the parent would marry again, in which case he or she was expected to resume the care of the children. Up to the middle of this century only children born in wedlock were eligible for the Müller Homes, but for several years now any child in need has been accepted.

There were three highlights in the year for the orphans: Mr. Müller's Birthday, on September 27th; Christmas; and the Pur Down Outing.

The Outing to Pur Down, a mile and a half from Ashley Down, was the Summer Treat from the earliest days. Everyone hoped and prayed for a fine day, though even when, as occasionally happened, rain started half way through the day, necessitating an early return, the orphans, unspoilt as they were, managed to keep cheerful and marched home literally 'singing in the rain'. The Outing began in the morning, every child carrying a little cotton bag hung round its neck on a tape, containing sweets and biscuits. The very simple picnic lunch and tea was conveyed to the field in large hampers, and the water for drinking was taken in a water cart loaned by Bristol Corporation. The children from the five Houses mixed freely as they pleased all day, and in the evening the Director and other leading people came to the field, and as the final event to mark the end of one more 'Pur Down', sent up five fire balloons, one for each House.

The Birthday Celebrations were marked for the orphans by the cake that was served; the only cake that was ever given to them in the regular way.

An old girl writes: 'We looked forward to the week in which the 27th came because we had a holiday. We used to go out most days, blackberry-picking. How we all enjoyed it!'

But of all the annual treats it was those connected with Christmas which called forth the most frequent and nostalgic references in letters written in after years by former orphans, now in their seventies and eighties. Here are some quotations from the *Reports* of the 1950's.

'Will you please use the enclosed £1 to buy something for those who do not receive parcels on Christmas Day. I hope they all have a good time. I was in Number 2 for seven years. I always enjoyed Christmas with all the games and putting up the decorations. I was very happy and enjoyed my stay there.'

'Well do I remember the happy Christmases spent at No. 4; the start of the preparations for the decorations; the arrival of the great, big Christmas tree, nothing on it, but I knew before Christmas it would be loaded with toys and presents; and somewhere amongst the many there would be one for me!'

(From 1928 *Report*.) 'I know that the children will be sure to have a very happy Christmas, being an old orphan myself, and I am always talking about the good old times gone by, when at the dear Homes.'

Many of the children had relatives who visited them and sent them letters, parcels and gifts of money, but others had no one belonging to them who ever took the least notice.

To remove some of this inequality, those who received money had to contribute a percentage into a common pool, to be shared out among the less privileged. Likewise at Christmas, those who received several parcels of toys had to give up some for those who were not so fortunate. This rule was naturally not much liked by those who had to part with what had been sent for what they regarded as their exclusive use, but as it was the unvarying custom no doubt they soon resigned themselves to the idea. Sharing was an obligation on which great stress was laid at Müller's.

Writing at Christmas time in 1930 one old orphan said, 'I expect the times are just as exciting as when I was there. I imagine the decorations being got ready, and the secrecy of it all, and then learning the lovely carols, and the Christmas Shop! I would love to peep in, to see if it is really like it used to be. I don't think it could possibly be better.' This 'Christmas Shop' refers to the little sweet shops which were opened in each wing of the Orphan Houses, in the earlier years at Christmas only, but later at other seasons as well. Each was managed by members of the staff of the school occupying that wing, and they bought the sweets from one or two large sweet manufacturers in Bristol and neighbourhood which offered them to the Ashley Down Orphanage on special terms. The general funds of the Institution were never used for this, but each wing had its own fund, built up from contributions made for the express purpose of providing treats for its children. In one of the old *Reports* a former orphan recalls that each child had been allowed to spend eightpence on sweets at Christmas. Everything in the Christmas Shops was sold at cost price, so no profit was made, but as the fund was constantly augmented by outside gifts there must usually have been a good deal in hand. Much of this was used to buy birthday and Christmas presents for those orphans who had no relatives to send them such things.

These little private shops typify George Müller's whole policy in the upbringing of the orphans, which was to keep them from the contamination of the world during their impressionable years. A hundred years ago those who ran orphanages had to evolve their own principles. There was little in the way of precedent to guide them, and less still of scientific understanding of child psychology. Nor could they read accounts of the success or failure of those who had attempted the same task before, as we can. Müller, one of the pioneers among orphanage-founders, had little else than his own experience in the matter to draw upon. His experience showed him that children who had come from very variable backgrounds nevertheless were happy and did well in what can only be described as the Orphan Hot-Houses. Kindly used, sheltered from a cruel world that had already treated many of them badly, trained by patient and conscientious teachers, in contact only with that which was pure and good, surrounded by children similarly shielded, most of them improved in health, manners and morals beyond all recognition. What Müller did not sufficiently realize was that it was this very protection which made it so difficult for many to adapt themselves to the world outside, when the inevitable moment came to 'stand forth on life's rough way'. Even those who were lucky enough to find themselves in a really good situation with understanding people were bound to feel the shock of the change; those who went to hard masters or mistresses must have had a bitter experience. Even the most commonplace activities such as doing household shopping or boarding a train must have been bewildering. It cannot have been easy either, for those who had always had a hundred familiar companions ready to hand, to know how to make friends with people of their own age in the outside world. In fact, they must have felt almost exactly like the Tristan Da Cunhans, flung forth from their uninhabitable island home, from a community one hundred per cent Christian, from a way of life simple, even hard, but stable, into the exciting, luxurious, noisy and semi-pagan world of mid-twentieth century Britain. A large number of orphans soon adapted themselves to their new life, settled down and did very well in the world, without losing what they had been taught at Ashley Down. No doubt it was these who tended to keep in touch with their old home and to bring themselves to Müller's notice on his travels. The failures would have been less eager to do so. There may not have been many of them, but one feels that there must have been some. Yet although the policy of thus shutting out the world and all its evil had such obvious disadvantages, it was one of the sources of the irresistible charm which the Orphan Houses had for many who were brought up in them, or who worked there. The spell seems to have lain on children and staff alike. As this century has advanced, this idea of keeping the orphans from all contact with the world has been progressively abandoned, until today the Müller children live in touch with life just like everyone else. But in consequence the inevitable has happened. The boys and girls take their places in the adult world with greater and greater ease, but the nostalgic references in the *Reports* to 'the dear old Home', 'the dearest place on earth to me', and so on, become fewer and fewer as the old generation dies off.

Any attempt to delineate the orphans' upbringing would be incomplete without reference being made to what is headed, in many of the *Reports* of the first quarter of the present century, 'Spiritual results.' The following paragraphs, quoted from some of these *Reports*, are certain to call forth reactions differing very much from one reader to another.

Report for 1931. 'It is the burden of earnest prayer daily that all the children brought in the Homes may become "the children of God by faith in Christ Jesus," and further, that they may develop stalwart Christian characters. Family worship is conducted morning and evening in each House, the course of reading leading regularly through the Old and New Testament Scriptures. Moreover, the children are encouraged to read the Bible for themselves... It is of peculiar interest and joy to learn how the children are drawn to the Saviour. Some have told me that some visitor brought the message which saved them; others say that one of their own teachers, or matrons, or nurses was the means of bringing them to see their need and accept the Saviour; others, again, speak of some boy or girl companion talking to them and leading them to Christ. No pressure is applied to get the children to make a profession of faith; our earnest aim and effort being to have a reality and a sane, healthy simplicity of Christian experience.'

Report for 1916, 'People are met with from time to time who say that they do not believe in child conversions. Thank God we *do* believe in them, and work definitely for that end; and God has given His blessing. There are today, engaged in the Institution, well over thirty workers who were formerly here as boys and girls; almost without exception these date their conversion to the days of their childhood; and their conduct proves the truth of their profession. It has been of interest to us, when bidding God speed to boys and girls leaving our care, to notice the variety of means God has been pleased to use in the conversion of some of these. A number have dated the change to the special services held by Mr. George Goodman, three and six years ago. Others mention special services held by Dr. Torrey. Some speak of decisions at prayer meetings amongst the children themselves, while not a few look back to the services in the various Houses, morning and evening, or on Sunday.'

A more detailed description is found on page 613 of the *Autobiography*, under the heading, *Revival among the Orphan Boys*. 'The following communication was sent to me,' writes George Müller, 'from our School Inspector, Mr. Horne: "February 9th, 1887: On January 15th, two boys came to one of the masters of No. 4, and asked if they might have a prayer meeting.

This request was granted. Several others met the same day, and on the next day (Sunday), the master on duty, seeing this desire for united prayer thus showing itself, told the boys, that he would not take them in class in the afternoon as usual, but that they might meet for prayer. About 150 thus met of their own accord for two hours. It is a frequent thing now for many, sometimes more than 100, to meet for prayer, after their evening meal, till school-time at seven. The work is mainly amongst the elder and more intelligent boys. One master said that they do their work better, their manners are softened, and some do not sulk, as they did before... Some boys, concerned about their souls, have come to a master and asked for help and instruction. Two came and said, 'Please, sir, to make us Christians.' Another said, 'My father, on his death-bed, made me promise to meet him in heaven, and I am not ready.' Last Sunday, all the boys above fourteen years, and who will be fourteen this year, were had by themselves and spoken to. There were about fifty-five, and of these, from thirty-five to forty professed faith in Christ; and there is nothing in their conduct to contradict their profession. Several boys have, of course, attended the meetings from curiosity only, and prayers were offered by the boys specially for such. A very marked feature in many boys is an earnest concern for the salvation of others. The whole tone of the school is changed.""'

Religious forcing-houses? Presumably the answer must be 'yes'. Brought up among adults to whom God was everything, to whom the life of faith was the only life worth living, the children naturally tended to absorb such beliefs, to emulate the Christian lives they saw being lived around them, to accept the truths that were taught them. There are scholastic forcing-houses; places where learning is in the atmosphere, where all that is noble and worthwhile in the world of books is held in reverence, where no effort is too great in order to attain an intimate knowledge of the classics. The same holds true of other spheres: music, art, athletics, and even the useful arts such as farming. Such environments are the main sources of supply of scholars, musicians, artists, athletes, farmers, as the case may be. They are all forcing-houses in their way, however indignantly those concerned may repudiate such a term. Scholars do occasionally come of illiterate parents, musicians and artists have been known to emerge from the most commonplace backgrounds, and there have certainly been saints of God who have grown up and lived out their lives amid depraved surroundings. But these exceptions only prove the rule, and those who look for the development of good learning, artistic talent or faith and holiness seek to nurture these things by the provision of the ideal environment, a good example and patient instruction.

George Müller and his associates, and their successors, concentrated upon providing for the orphans the ideal setting for the growth of faith; they set them the best possible example, they taught them, they prayed for them to that end. Those youthful professions of faith were a beginning, but it was the lives lived to the very end in that same faith that proved its reality. The letters quoted below, and the life stories related in the next chapter, show that the forcing-house, if such it was, could produce some robust blooms.

'My father, now in his 88th year, asks me to send you this donation of £1 towards your work among boys and girls. Himself once a Müller's boy, he spent eight years in the Homes, and recollects the love and care showered on a young lad without home or parents. In the eventide of life he looks back and appreciates those who not only cared for his material needs but were careful to make sure that he was instructed in the Christian way of life which proved such a sure foundation for later days.'

'I was once in great need and Müller's Orphan Homes opened their protecting doors to me. The loving care and Christian teaching I received there I can never forget, neither can I ever hope to repay. The life and work and faith of George Müller is an abiding influence in my life for which I humbly thank God.'

'Praise God for all the memories of the years I spent at the dear Orphan Homes. Truly God's Word is a lamp until my feet and a light unto my path. Your old Orphan Boy.'

The following is part of a letter received by Mr. Wright in 1902. 'I am not personally acquainted with you, but as the successor to the benefactor of my youth, the good George Müller, you are and ever will be dear to me, one of the earliest Orphan Boys at No. 3, Wilson Street, Bristol. I am now seventy-two years of age, and for about forty years have never slept without remembering my early friend, and the Orphan Houses, at the Throne of Grace.'

CHAPTER FIFTEEN

SOME OF THE ORPHANS

It may help to throw further light on life in the Homes, on how the children reacted to it, and also on their opportunities after leaving, if the stories of a few individual orphans who managed to carve out successful careers for themselves are related.

Although their names cannot now be traced, mention must be made of the first two boys admitted after the opening of Number 1 in

1849. They were two brothers, evidently of unusual intelligence and character. One became a clergyman of the Church of England, and the other a Congregational deacon and a local preacher.

Then there was William Ready, whose story can be given in detail, from facts obtained from his biography by Lewis L. Court, called *Ready, aye Ready*. William was the youngest of the ten children of an Irish monumental mason living in London. Drink led to the father's failure in business and to the downfall of the family. William was born in a workhouse, and was orphaned of both parents by the age of five. He was then nominally under the care of an elder brother, who was addicted to drink and who terrorized him. For several years he led the life of a street arab, picking up a living as best he could as a shoeblack, performing acrobatics for pennies, sleeping in dustbins.

Then a London City Missionary noticed the resourceful boy, by that time leader of the gang, and determined to reclaim him. The first time he laid hold of him the lad escaped, but the second time he held him fast, led him home, fed and clothed him, and managed to prevent him from slipping off again, while corresponding with George Müller. The upshot of all this was that William arrived one day at the Orphan Houses, was put into uniform, and found himself for the first time in his life under discipline. Needless to say, the wild youngster, with his Irish blood, did not take at all kindly to the life, and twice ran away. He was also very insubordinate, and was the despair of the masters. Even the boys at times thought that he had gone too far. He settled down better after a time, but even so was glad when the time came to be apprenticed. He was extremely fortunate in his master, a miller of fatherly disposition and saintly life. It was not very long before Ready was himself converted, and a few years later he became a Free Church Minister. Later he went to New Zealand, where he had a long and distinguished career. He died in 1927.

Of his time at the Orphan Houses, he wrote later in life, 'Did I dislike the place? It was not exactly that, but I felt all the time I was in the orphanage just like a bird in a cage. I was craving for liberty and the wide world. I can see now that it was just the place for me and what a blessing it was that I was sent there. If my own children were left orphans I could wish nothing better for them than that they should be trained and cared for at Müller's.' He also wrote, 'How vividly comes back to my mind that last meeting with the father of the fatherless before leaving his care! He received me kindly when I went into his prayer room at No. 3 Orphanage. Ah! What wonderful prayers had been offered there on behalf of the orphans, and what wonderful answers he had there received.'

What follows is quoted from Court's book. 'Müller put half a crown into his left hand and a Bible in his right and said, "You can hold tighter with your right hand than with your left, can you not?" He answered, "Yes, sir." "Well, my lad, hold to the teaching of that Book and you will always have something for your left hand to hold." He then asked the lad to kneel, and putting his hands on his head, he committed him to the keeping of the Heavenly Father. Then raising him, he said, "Trust in the Lord and do good; so shalt thou dwell in the land and verily thou shalt be fed"; and then "Good-bye". "So I left the school. My belongings were my Bible, my clothes and half a crown, and what is best of all, the priceless blessing of George Müller's prayers."'

Thomas Millidge's father was a master-bootmaker, and his mother the daughter of a merchant sea captain. He was born posthumously in 1858 in Guildford. His mother died little more than a year later, but before she died she expressed a wish that her son should be taken to George Müller so that his Christian upbringing might be assured. The little boy was brought to Ashley Down at the age of two, and remained there virtually for the rest of his life. He proved to be intelligent, and instead of being sent out as an apprentice, was made a Pupil Teacher under the scheme started in 1873. After the usual period of training at

232

Purton School, he returned to become a permanent member of the staff of the Orphan Houses. For many years he was a master at Number 4, and later in life exchanged this post for that of secretary of the department dealing with the purchasing of stores. He died at the age of 88. These facts were told to me by his son, Captain L. Millidge, retired after a lifetime in the Merchant Navy. Many hundreds of orphans must have known Mr. Millidge, and affectionate references to his memory are frequent in their letters.

Here is one from the 1944 *Report*: 'Well do I remember Mr. Millidge as a young man. I was a boy in No. 1, and he was one of the masters of No. 4; and sometimes he came over as relief when one of our masters was either ill or on holiday. How the boys used to crowd round him, because he entered into their games and made himself as one of them.'

Fanny Roberta White entered the Homes in 1879, and during her first year was brought to the Lord. She went to domestic work in Bath, and later trained as a missionary and went out to China, where she met and married T. J. Underwood, of the Baptist Missionary Society. In 1900 they were taken prisoners by the Boxers, and five days later were executed.

There have been many marriages between Old Boys and Old Girls of the Homes, but that of the Tidballs must surely be one of the most

233

romantic.

Mr. William Tidball was born in 1882, and entered the Orphan House when he was six years old. He left at fourteen to be apprenticed to a printer in Carmarthen. As already related, he was unfortunate in his master, but nevertheless stuck to his trade, and when his apprenticeship was finished he took a job in Sheffield. There he spent all his working life, and also his married life with his first wife. The story of his second marriage forms part of Mrs. Tidball's life story, which is here told mainly in her own words as she gave it to me, when I visited them at their comfortable home in Horfield, Bristol, in 1958.

'In the year 1888 I (Ellen Petherick as she was then) was taken to Müller's No. 1 Orphan House on September 21st, with my sister. I was sixteen months old, and could not walk or speak, I was so frail. I was put into Mr. Müller's arms by my grandmother, who took us there from Exeter. I have been told by my teachers that I was so weak and frail that I was always carried about on a pillow. I was in the Nursery until I was six, needing special care under a dear old nurse, who I remember was very fond of me. As I grew, being so frail and small I was called "Spider", and that name stuck to me for many years, but, praise God, I am much more than a spider now, through His goodness, and kindness to me of His servants.

In 1893 the Infant girls from No. 1 were divided out to the other houses, as it was going to be used for small boys. Over at No. 2 I did not seem to be understood by the teachers, as I had been such a pet in No. 1. I always seemed to be getting into scrapes and punishment. I suppose I was stronger then and was enjoying life in my way. 1896 I was transferred back to No. 1 Girls' school, where my sister was one of the older girls. It was nice to have her to go to and tell my troubles, but the time came when she passed on to the Domestic Department, so I had my difficulties to fight myself. At about the age of thirteen years, I was not a Christian, but I well remember in the playground, a group of us girls were talking over such things (as we often did), when I said I would give my heart to the Lord, and although not apparent in my behaviour, as I was still full of fun and laughter, I still feel that is when I became the Lord's. You must realize that with 110 of you it was difficult always to be good, and I was a real pickle.

'Now at the age of 15 years it was time to pass on to the Domestic Department, where for a few months we were with the infant boys, generally looking after them, washing the small ones, and scrubbing and cleaning their dormitories and other rooms. Later we passed up to the Kitchen and Laundry Department, until it was time for us to leave at the age of seventeen. I wondered what sort of a situation would be found for me. In 1904, about the age of sixteen and a half years, the Matron told me that I was to go to the Sick Infirmary, and to help nurse the children, as scarlet fever had broken out, and the nurse of the Infirmary was isolated with them in another ward.' This led to Ellen Petherick being trained first under Miss Bergin, who had started the system of keeping suitable girls on for sick-nurse training, instead of their being sent into service in the usual way.

She had observed the girl's aptitude for nursing. 'I was told to go over and see the Directors. When I arrived at No. 3, Mr. Bergin and his daughter put me at my ease and had a talk with me. I was asked if I would like to take up nursing. I said "Yes", but was told to go and pray and think it over (the first big step in my life). After two or three days I told Miss Bergin I would like to do so.' Ellen Petherick worked in the Infirmaries of the Homes until she was twenty-two, and then left to train at a Plymouth Hospital. After three years she became run down in health, and went first to a farm in the country to rest, and then to a married sister. While there, Miss Bergin wrote inviting her to return to the Homes. She did so, and 'Sister Petherick' remained on the staff of the Homes for forty years.

'In May, 1951, the Directors called the staff for a meeting, (there were about twenty of us)

236

to tell us that the nature of the work was changing, and it would be Scattered Homes, and as we would not all be needed then, we could look out for what we thought would suit us, but they did not wish to let us down in any way. After the meeting, the Staff got together, and it was said to me, "Sister, what are you going to do?" I said, "Pray for a home and a husband—and if it could be a former orphan boy..." They laughed, but I did this.

'Now see how the Lord answers the prayers of those who *do* put their trust in Him, believing. On September 9th, I went over to No. 3 just to have a chat with the Matron. She looked out of the window and said, "There is a gentleman walking from Lodge to Lodge, I wonder what he wants!" I said, "I am going back to No. 5 I will ask him if I can help him." So down to the Lodge I trotted in nurse's uniform. He came forward and raised his hat. I said, "Can I help you?" He said, "You certainly can. I am a former No. 4 boy." I said, "I am a former No. 1 girl." We then shook hands. He told me the names of his masters. Mr. Packer and Mr. Millidge were the ones he thought of most. He had come all the way from Sheffield to stay with a cousin, as he had lost his wife in May. After taking him up to see Mr. Ronald Packer, who could tell him out of a big book when he came to No. 4 and where he went as apprentice... I gave him a cup of tea. Before leaving he said that he would like to write to me when he got back to Sheffield.' They met and corresponded a few times, became engaged before the end of the year, and were married in the following June, the Directors and their wives giving a reception for them at No. 3. Their photograph, complete with wedding cake, appeared in the *Report* for 1953.

Edith Larby has written her own account of her life, under the title of *Nothing Impossible*. She was at Ashley Down after George Müller's time. Her father, a gardener, found that he could not cope with three small girls when their mother had died, and placed them in the Müller Homes when Edith was nearly seven years old. She says that she did not take kindly to lessons or routine, missing the old freedom of a country home, but she got on well with the other children. She never really became adjusted to the institution life, and was rebellious and troublesome throughout her schooldays and in her first situation afterwards. As a child her favourite pastime had been to play at being a hospital nurse, and this developed into a serious ambition as she grew older. In her second situation, which was in a doctor's household, she was given every help and encouragement to enter the Nursing Profession. She became a State Registered Nurse and gained her C.M.B. In 1927 she found Christ, and thenceforward her work as a nurse was done in His service.

Eventually, after years of private nursing, she opened her own little maternity home, with the help of one of her sisters and a friend, both genuine Christians.

Then mention must be made of Mr. Lewis F. Gobey who came to Müller's at the age of six with two brothers and two sisters, in 1901. He was placed in No. 4 Infant Boys' Department, moving up two years later into the Millidge older boys' school, where he spent five happy years. Mr. Millidge was Senior Master (equivalent to Headmaster), and both he and his assistants were men of sound Christian faith and life. Mr. Gobey told me that it was this which made for the happy atmosphere of the school.

On his fourteenth birthday in 1908 Lewis Gobey became a pupil teacher, and, after five years, a junior master. By August, 1916, however, he was in the army, and on his way to the Middle East, where he served in the Royal Veterinary Corps as a clerk. Demobilized in 1919, he got into touch with his old school, and was quickly induced to return as assistant master to No. 4, where there was an acute staff shortage. He remained there for the rest of his working life, and was Senior Master from 1944 to 1950. Then the school department of the Homes was closed, and the children began to go out to the local primary and secondary schools. Mr. Gobey stayed on as House Master up to the last day of the work on Ashley Down, when having conducted the remaining twenty-two children to their new home at Ashley Down House, Cotham, and handed them over to their new House Master, his work was finished, and he entered upon his retirement. Hundreds of boys passed through his hands during his forty-three years on the staff at Müller's, and many an old boy will remember him with affection. His is another instance of old boy marrying old girl. His wife, Miss Nelly Cummins in her unmarried days, was in No. 2. House.

The three extracts from *Reports* which follow, and which reveal the lasting influence of the Orphan Houses on the lives and characters of the orphans, bring this book to a close.

1918. 'The master of one of our former orphans writes, telling of this lad's death in France: "He had witnessed brightly for the Lord amidst unbridled ungodliness, and gained victories through 'Lessons first learnt at Ashley Down'." The master writes as one who has lost a dearly-loved son.'

1931. 'I think it right to let you know of the death of E.M.H. She passed away last month. She was brought up in your Orphanage, and came to me when she was seventeen years of age. After some years she became my housekeeper, and was in my employ thirty-four years. She was a most sincere Christian.

Baptized by the late Mr. F. B. Meyer, she was faithful and consistent in all her ways, and as near faultless as any human being could be. She was like a sister or a daughter. I have entertained many ministers for the day. Miss H. was always thought highly of by them all. After her death the well-known evangelist who for years sat at my table on the Lord's day wrote and said she was the most faultless woman he had met with in his travels. "You may know some faults in her," he said. I told him I did not; and that during the thirty-four years she had been in my employ not one cross word had passed between us. Such a life speaks well for the early Christian training she had in your Homes.'

1910. 'From an Old Boy, 10s. This young man left us eleven years ago to be apprenticed to a tailor. Five years later he joined the Navy, and has just returned from two-and-a-half years' commission in the China Sea. His first visit was to Bristol, to see his former masters at No. 4 New Orphan House. In converse with them he mentioned that another old No. 4 boy was on the same ship with him, and many were the quiet talks they had together about the old Home at Ashley Down. One Sunday evening at Hong Kong, when both were leaning silently over the side of the ship, a noisy boatload of sailors returned from what they called "a jollification" on shore, and this Old Boy then asked his companion what kept them from that sort of thing, pointing to the boat. "Ashley Down," promptly replied the other, adding, "and the influence of the old Home has been our sheet-anchor all through.'"

Photoset, printed and bound in Great Britain by
REDWOOD PRESS LIMITED, Melksham, Wiltshire

TANGLEWOOD

✓